Likenesses of Truth

Likenesses of Truth in Elizabethan and Restoration Drama

HARRIETT HAWKINS

Oxford AT THE CLARENDON PRESS
1972

Oxford University Press, Ely House, London W. 1

GLASGOW NEW YORK TORONTO MELBOURNE WELLINGTON
CAPE TOWN IBADAN NAIROBI DAR ES SALAAM LUSAKA ADDIS ABABA
DELHI BOMBAY CALCUTTA MADRAS KARACHI LAHORE DACCA
KUALA LUMPUR SINGAPORE HONG KONG TOKYO

PRINTED IN GREAT BRITAIN
AT THE UNIVERSITY PRESS, OXFORD
BY VIVIAN RIDLER
PRINTER TO THE UNIVERSITY

For Robert W. Hawkins

'A life well acted is the sweetest remembrance.'

The purity of phrase, the clearness of conception and expression, the boldness maintained to majesty, the significancy and sound of words, not strained into bombast, but justly elevated; in short, those very words and thoughts, which cannot be changed, but for the worse, must of necessity escape our transient view upon the theatre; and yet without all these a play may take. For if either the story move us, or the actor help the lameness of it with his performance, or now and then a glittering beam of wit or passion strike through the obscurity of the poem, any of these are sufficient to effect a present liking, but not to fix a lasting admiration; for nothing but truth can long continue; and time is the surest judge of truth.   DRYDEN

Preface

I see a thing vively presented on the *Stage* . . . by the Poet, as I can therein view the daily examples of mens lives, and images of Truth, in their manners, so drawne for my delight, or profit, as I may (either way) use them.   BEN JONSON

THIS survey of dramatic perspectives in a number of Elizabethan and Jacobean plays, and in three Restoration comedies, is designed to demonstrate (or at least to argue) that the truths embodied in these examples of great imaginative literature are not just imaginative visions of reality, but that they are truths about human experience which have been explored and exhibited in different ways by different kinds of artists. The Elizabethan plays were selected for discussion because they deal so explicitly with facts about the drama itself (*The Spanish Tragedy*, *A Midsummer Night's Dream*, *The Tempest*); with social and ethical truths which, as I shall argue, are subsequently falsified by a contrived ending (*Measure for Measure*); and with differing tragic and moral truths (*Romeo and Juliet*, *Julius Caesar*, *Macbeth*, *King Lear*). The three Restoration comedies (*The Man of Mode*, *Love for Love*, and *The Way of the World*) were chosen because they all so effectively combine, in differing ways, an emphasis on facts about the presentation of self in everyday social life with an emphasis on facts about the dramatic presentation of characters on the stage.

Along with this defence of the drama's claim to truth goes a polemical attack on certain modern critical fictions. By trying to find some abstract moral order operating in tragedy and comedy alike, for instance, some very influential modern criticism has substituted moral criteria for dramatic criteria in its evaluation of characters, and thus imposed a relatively easy moral idealism upon the dramatic presentation of certain hard facts about human experience. A related critical fiction is the notion that an ideal 'Elizabethan audience' would have, should have, or could have done the same thing. The need to liberate discussions of seventeenth-century plays from the shackles which specific modern critical perspectives have clamped upon them calls for a frontal attack on specific critics. At this point in time, it seems particularly important to challenge currently fashionable views of these plays because several of them are being taught as orthodox ones in schools, while others are frequently taken for granted in critical introductions to popular editions of the texts. But the major purpose here is not to assail a group of twentieth-century critics. Rather it is to show that while some of the greatest plays written in the seventeenth century remain, by their own definitions, 'nothing but shadows', 'insubstantial pageants', or 'fabulous counterfeits', they simultaneously have triumphantly survived the test of time, and remain original likenesses of human experience. And from a consideration of the plays themselves perhaps it is possible to conclude that by confronting our own illusions with their more accurate images of the tragic and comic ways of this world—and by thus enabling us to accept, to enjoy, or to endure, things as they really are—the playwrights perform their most significant act of instruction.

ACKNOWLEDGEMENTS

Much of this book was written while I held generous summer grants from the Folger Shakespeare Library, the National Endowment for the Humanities, and the Henry E. Huntington Library. Most of Chapter II has been published in *Shakespeare Studies* (1972), and an informal lecture that included portions of Chapter VII was printed in *The Maryland English Journal* (spring 1968).

I am deeply indebted to R. M. Adams and J. B. Bamborough, who read preliminary drafts of the manuscript and gave me helpful suggestions.

The quotations from Shakespeare follow the text of *The Complete Works of Shakespeare*, edited by Peter Alexander, and quotations from Congreve follow *The Complete Plays of William Congreve*, edited by Herbert Davis.

H. H.

Vassar College
June 1971

Contents

Contents

1 Introduction: some dramatic and critical illusions and realities

All advance of scientific understanding, at every level, begins with a speculative adventure, an imaginative preconception *of what might be true*—a preconception which always, and necessarily, goes a little way (sometimes a long way) beyond anything which we have logical or factual authority to believe in. It is the invention of a Possible World, or of a tiny fraction of that world. The conjecture is then exposed to criticism to find out whether or not that imagined world is anything like the real one. Scientific reasoning is therefore at all levels an interaction between two episodes of thought, a dialogue between two voices, the one imaginative and the other critical; a dialogue, if you like, between the possible and the actual, between proposal and disposal, conjecture and criticism; between what might be true and what is in fact the case. . . .Would it not be reasonable to say that literary criticism has a function cognate with that which I have attributed to criticism in science?

P. B. MEDAWAR, 'Science & Literature'

NEAR the end of *The Tempest*, Prospero, who years earlier had neglected worldly ends in favour of 'art' and philosophical speculation—and thereby lost his dukedom to Antonio—abruptly ends his revels of the imagination, stops his masque, banishes his spirits, and directs his attention to Caliban's conspiracy against his life:

> I had forgot that foul conspiracy
> Of the beast Caliban and his confederates
> Against my life; the minute of their plot
> Is almost come. [*To the Spirits*] Well done; avoid; no more!

Shakespeare's supreme dramatic 'god of power' has to turn from the realm of his imagination, of his art, to confront a physical threat from brute nature. And time after time, in Elizabethan drama, there comes some such moment of truth when a character identified with supreme human power, whether it be the power of the crown or the power of art, is confronted by certain facts of ordinary life, by some empirical truth which no power of royalty, intelligence, or imagination can alter, and which therefore must be taken into account. In the Elizabethan drama the Roman reminder, 'Remember thou art only a man', is a warning issued to kings, magicians, and scholars alike:

Alexander. Why then doest thou owe no reverence to Kings?
Diogenes. No.
Alexander. Why so?
Diogenes. Because they be no Gods.
Alexander. They be Gods of the earth.
Diogenes. Yea, Gods of earth.

Alexander. I have the world at command.
Diogenes. And I in contempt.
Alexander. Thou shalt live no longer than I will.
Diogenes. But I will die whether you will or no.

Lyly's Alexander has to face the fact that what he can will is limited by what will happen in the course of things. He finds that he can no more command human nature and order Campaspe to love him than he can alter the course of external nature and order Diogenes not to die. King Lear learns that royalty could not command (or buy) genuine love from his children any more than it could order the thunder to peace at its bidding (IV. vi. 97–107). Facing his moment of truth, as midnight approaches, Dr. Faustus realizes that he can no longer, by will or by imagination, control or ignore the literal facts that 'The stars move still, time runs, the clock will strike'. After continually retreating into fantasies about the crown and about himself, King Richard II finally admits that his royal imagination cannot tear a passage through prison walls, that he bears a burden like an ass, spurred and galled by jouncing Bolingbroke. Then, after these recognitions, when the physical embodiments of Bolingbroke's power arrive to assassinate him, Richard goes down courageously, fighting them on their own level, while his soul mounts up, royally, above it all.

Conversely, the advocates or exponents of factual reality in some of these plays have to come to grips with imaginative, emotional, or symbolic truths. Caliban finally recognizes Pros-

pero's supreme power, and in the same scene the practical old
politician, Alonso, recognizes the mystery embodied in Prospero:
'there is in this business more than nature / Was ever conduct of.'
King Richard's antagonist and opposite, Bolingbroke, who knew
from the outset that no imagination of a feast could 'cloy the
hungry edge of appetite', emotionally and imaginatively confronts the personal and symbolic consequences of his action, and
hopes to make a pilgrimage to the Holy Land to atone for his
own crimes and to avert, if he can, Carlisle's prophecy that all of
England will yet groan because he took the crown from the true
King. And for Dr. Faustus the literal fact that he cannot stop time
is overshadowed by his horror at the cosmic and emotional
realities which the course of time and the truth of nature reflect:

> All beasts are happy, for when they die
> Their souls are soon dissolved in elements.
> But mine must live still to be plagued in hell!
> Cursed be the parents that engendered me!
> No Faustus, curse thyself, curse Lucifer
> That hath deprived thee of the joys of heaven.
> *The clock strikes twelve*

These works, then, combine an emphasis on human power
with a critical analysis of the limits of this power. One might
argue that in some of these plays the dramatic action reflects the
fundamental clash between two equally valid kinds of truth which
ideally should be integrated but which frequently fail (in art and
literary criticism alike) to take each other into account—a clash
between the moral and psychological truth of human experience
and the empirical, literal, factual truth about human experience.
Certainly the confrontation between these mighty opposites frequently has great dramatic power:

> *Hamlet.*   Do you see nothing there?
> *Queen.*   Nothing at all; yet all that is I see.

But from another point of view the two levels of truth may be
seen to co-operate with each other (like Don Quixote and Sancho
Panza) within the total contexts of certain plays in which they
appear, to combine in and be encompassed by the total truth

conveyed by the individual plays. For the plays themselves stress both kinds of truth and in doing so they fuse them in the attention and the memory of the audience:

Lady Macbeth. A little water clears us of this deed.   (II. ii. 67)

Lady Macbeth. Yet who would have thought the old man to have had so much blood in him? . . . .What, will these hands ne'er be clean?
(v. i. 37–42)

Why does this confrontation-combination of two kinds of truth occur with such frequency in the Elizabethan drama? The contemporary emphasis on both the literal and the spiritual (imaginative, figurative, symbolic) truths of the Scriptures may have provoked thought as to when, where, and whether these levels of truth conflicted with or reinforced each other. The popular conception of the world as a stage certainly inspired playwrights to analyse the relationships between the truths of their imaginative worlds and the truths of the real one. And the private experience of the playwrights themselves may have produced an ironic awareness of the difference between their vast power in the realms of art and imagination and their limited powers in ordinary life. Within the theatrical world of his imagination, for instance, the young genius, Christopher Marlowe, could be a mighty god, sending his favoured creation and spokesman, Tamburlaine, thundering across Asia and overcoming all obstacles on his way to an ultimate ride in triumph through Persepolis. In the first part of *Tamburlaine* neither the author nor his hero admits any limits to his will or to his freedom to act in accordance with that will. But in the second part, the foremost limit imposed upon the human condition presents itself. In the course of nature Zenocrate, then Tamburlaine himself, must die. And Tamburlaine dies knowing that for a god of earth there will always be worlds left unconquered:

> And from th' Antarctic Pole eastward behold
> As much more land, which never was descried,
> Wherein are rocks of pearl that shine as bright
> As all the lamps that beautify the sky!
> And I shall die, and this unconquered?

Now Marlowe himself, Marlowe the man who died in a tavern fight at twenty-nine, not only faced the same ultimate limit to human will; he also faced some very mundane limits on human freedom from which he could release his creation, Tamburlaine.[1] Unlike his hero, Marlowe seems to have been plagued and tormented by all the everyday, ordinary limits on personal freedom; by conventional morality, by conventional wisdom and dogma, by toil, envy, want, the patron, and the gaol. And Marlow's greatest play, *Dr. Faustus*, continually reminds us of the essentially cruel limits which the human condition, by its very nature, imposes upon even the freest of free wills. Faustus, who (like all of us) wants to will what in the nature of things cannot be willed, can only exchange one set of limitations for another, can only exchange the limitations imposed by Heaven for the limitations imposed by Hell. With bitter pity and personal terror Marlowe shows us how the dice are loaded against the hero. His freedom to conjure is limited if he does not conjure, and he is (damned) limited if he does.[2] Furthermore, to make any choice at all inevitably precludes the freedom of simultaneously making the opposite choice. In *Dr. Faustus* the dream of ultimate freedom is presented as a tragically hollow illusion. With increasing desperation, Faustus retreats from the recognition of the limits imposed upon him by escaping into ever more potent and addictive illusions. In order to forget the facts which he acknowledged in the beginning—the fact that he is 'still but Faustus, and a man', and the fact that he cannot free himself from the consequences of his own decisions and desires—Faustus indulges in fantasies ranging from the grotesquely trivial dance of the Seven Deadly Sins to the damning kiss from a demon in the form of Helen of

[1] The idea of the creation, the work of art, which is free from the limits imposed upon its vulnerable human creator is the subject of some great Romantic and modern poetry. See Frank Kermode, *The Romantic Image* (London, 1957).

[2] Dorothy Parker gives us some similarly (and relevantly) loaded dice in her poem 'Partial Comfort':

> Whose love is given over well,
> Shall gaze on Helen's face in Hell.
> Whilst they whose love is thin and wise
> May view John Knox in Paradise.

Troy.[3] Furthermore, Faustus's power itself is an illusion. Like Marlowe, who could not claim the power of a historical Tamburlaine, Faustus cannot command the real Alexander; he can only summon up a spirit-actor in the form of Alexander. Faustus, like Marlowe, can only put on the shows of power. Like Marlowe's art, the power of Faustus's art is effective only in the realm of the imagination. When finally facing empirical reality, Faustus's mighty poetic lines—Marlowe's lines—change from the imperative 'will' ('I will conjure') to the inevitable 'will' ('the clock will strike')—from '*I* will' to '*It* will'. And where Faustus commanded Lucifer and Mephistophilis to come to him in the beginning, he cannot stop them from coming to take total dominion over him in the end. Significantly, the illusions summoned by Faustus himself and the illusions sent to him from Hell are frequently identical. In more ways than one, Faustus is the tragic victim of his own illusions. And do Faustus's alternatives—contrition, prayer, repentance—really offer a way to transcend the human condition, or do they merely offer yet another set of illusions?

Faustus.	Contrition, prayer, repentance, what of these?
Good Angel.	O, they are means to bring thee unto heaven.
Bad Angel.	Rather illusions, fruits of lunacy,
	That make men foolish that do use them most.

There is always the possibility—and Marlowe daringly poses it— that *any* idealism, just like any diabolism, which offers an escape from the limits of the human condition 'begets a world of idle fantasies'.

On a secular level, and over and over again—from *Love's Labour's Lost* to *The Tempest*—Marlowe's successor, the most supremely imaginative poet of all, depicts escapist withdrawals into fantasy, abstraction, and speculation either as comic follies or as tragic dangers that must be exposed as such unless and until they can be subjected to or reinforced by the test of empirical reality. In *Love's Labour's Lost* Shakespeare shows us the comic futility of Ferdinand's philosophical warfare against human bio-

---

[3] When he makes the spirit-demon in the form of Helen his paramour, Faustus commits the act of demoniality, that is, bodily intercourse with demons. See W. W. Greg, 'The Damnation of Faustus', *MLR*, xli (1946), 97–107.

logy and human affections. Then he shows us the illusory nature of an idealistic Courtly Love which sees the symbol (the jewel on the sleeve) instead of the thing symbolized (the real Princess behind her vizard). Human beings, Shakespeare implies, make themselves as ridiculous when they pretend to transcend their humanity—their affections, their biology, their social necessity—as any imp pretending to be great Hercules or any curate pretending to be Alexander. For the literal truths of biology, social necessity, and human affections can shatter all such pretensions in a single minute:

> Princess.   Welcome, Marcade;
>   But that thou interruptest our merriment.
> Marcade.   I am sorry, madam; for the news I bring
>   Is heavy in my tongue. The King your father—
> Princess.   Dead, for my life!
> Marcade.   Even so; my tale is told.
> Berowne.   Worthies, away; the scene begins to cloud.

Then we are poignantly reminded of the limits of comic art. We learn that it is impossible to 'move wild laughter in the throat of death', that wit and mirth 'cannot move a soul in agony', and that the stuff of life itself cannot be wholly confined within the limits of conventional comic form:

> Berowne.   Our wooing doth not end like an old play:
>   Jack hath not Jill. These ladies' courtesy
>   Might well have made our sport a comedy.
> King.   Come, sir, it wants a twelvemonth an' a day,
>   And then 'twill end.
> Berowne.   That's too long for a play.

And so the 'words of Mercury' counterpoint the 'songs of Apollo' from the very beginning of Shakespeare's career.

Later, within the historical framework of *Richard II*, Shakespeare shows us Richard sheltering himself from the threat of Bolingbroke by retreating into private fantasies, by overdramatizing various situations, by depending upon the symbolical power of the crown to protect him until it is too late for him to protect the real crown. Still later, Prospero says that he once made a rather similar withdrawal into the realms of private speculation and (like Richard) he lost his real kingdom. But Prospero does not make the same mistake again. He deals very directly with Caliban. And ultimately Prospero seems to solve the problem which Dr. Faustus could not solve by freely admitting and accepting the limits of his magical power. For Shakespeare's most omnipotent dramatic 'god of power' defines himself, frankly, as a god of earth. The words of Mercury are communicated through the very song of Apollo when Prospero admits that his beautiful masque is a vanity of his art, an insubstantial pageant, and when Prospero admits that once his show is over his personal strength is faint, that he is growing old, and that henceforth his every third thought will be of his grave. In a mysterious way, when he intellectually, imaginatively, and emotionally accepts the limits of his power, Prospero frees himself from its limits; and somehow, by acknowledging and accepting the limits of the human condition, Prospero seems to surmount them. Here, if ever, a supreme work of the human imagination may be seen to encompass an analysis of the limits of the human imagination and, in doing so, to transcend them.

Thus, throughout his career (and with great sympathy and power) Shakespeare tries to show us that fantasy and speculation divorced from the truths of human experience and human emotion are comically and tragically hollow. At the very same time, he shows us that without the powers of human imagination and intellect the empirical and emotional facts of life can neither be assimilated nor controlled. And Shakespeare's great contemporary, Ben Jonson, repeatedly and explicitly reaches exactly the same conclusions: 'The true Artificer will not run away from nature, as hee were afraid of her; or depart from life, and the likenesse of Truth . . . without Art, Nature can ne're bee perfect; &, without Nature, Art can clayme no being.'[4] For while they do so by very different methods, Jonson's comedy, *The Alchemist*, and his masque, *Mercury Vindicated from the Alchemists*, illustrate the same ideas which Shakespeare exhibits in *The Tempest*. Where

---

[4] Quotations are from *Discoveries*, in *Ben Jonson*, ed. C. H. Herford and Percy and Evelyn Simpson, vol. viii (Oxford, 1947), ll. 772–4, 2503–4.

Shakespeare shows us that Prospero's art, while 'abounding in the loftiest mysteries', also embraces 'the affinity of all nature', Jonson shows us that alchemy (his dramatic metaphor for false arts of all kinds in both works) 'can claim the name neither of art nor science'. It is vain and empty precisely because it tries to defy the truth of nature;[5] whereas true art, like his own play about alchemy, gives us a likeness of truth that never departs from the facts of London life which it enhances and so enjoyably displays.

'Experience, Observation, Sense, Induction, are the fower Tryers of Arts. It is ridiculous to teach anything for undoubted Truth, that Sense, and Experience, can confute.'[6] So says Ben Jonson. And indeed the best Elizabethan dramatists constantly subject the products of their imagination to the tests of sense and experience. But all too often, influential modern criticism fails to apply the same tests to its own imaginative constructions. Where the drama simultaneously reflects both emotional realities and literal truths some modern critics limit their emphasis to one or the other, and we get discussions of, say, *Othello*, which deny the existence of its emotional realities, ignore the sheer pity and terror evoked by the tragic hero, for the sake of a catalogue of his failure to conduct himself in accord with ideal moral standards. Of course the counter-argument that we should appreciate characters 'emotionally', or sympathize with their 'human dilemmas', might appear to be an argument that we should abandon any strict critical standards at all. And this might be an acceptable demurral if we were dealing with some other form of literary or perhaps non-literary art. But there are special circumstances in the drama, whereby the work of art, if it does not appeal to a number of people on a personal, emotional level, may be precisely nothing. The playwrights themselves very obviously recognize their obligation (and their power) to 'move' their audiences. Sometimes they may even resort to melodrama and sentimentality in order to do so. For if a play's major thrust, its major emotional impact, is not

---

[5] The distinction between true and false 'arts' is neatly defined by Pico della Mirandola in his oration, *Of the Dignity of Man*, tr. E. L. Forbes, *Journal o the History of Ideas*, iii (1942), 353.

[6] Jonson, Preface to *The English Grammar, Ben Jonson*, viii, ll. 12–14.

communicated to the audience before it leaves the theatre, the play will fail. All the plays to be discussed here have held the stage for several hundred years; and in order to do so they have had to appeal to all kinds of people besides scholars, graduate students, and literary critics. And thus when modern criticism substitutes moral criteria for dramatic criteria in evaluating these plays and their characters, it runs the danger of ignoring the essential nature of the theatre itself. Furthermore, the pervasively moral idealism of some influential modern criticism (by its very nature) has fixed essentially the same, unnecessarily limited and rigid critical point of view upon radically differing plays, radically differing authors, and radically differing characters.

In recent years, by far the most fashionable critical perspective on all sorts of characters who appear in seventeenth-century plays—such diverse characters as Isabella, Romeo, Dorimant, and Millamant—is the diagnostic, severely righteous, highly critical perspective of a satirist rather like Marston's Malevole, who formally castigates the vices and follies of the characters within his domain. Now while there is no doubt that a detached, derisive, point of view is exactly the right one to adopt towards the vast majority of characters in *The Malcontent*, *Volpone*, and *The Revenger's Tragedy* (or rather it is demonstrably the right one because it is precisely the point of view which the playwrights and their official spokesmen themselves adopt), it is a point of view which precludes any full appreciation of the characters caught in the emotionally charged first half of *Measure for Measure* (Chapter III) or any full enjoyment of Etherege's Dorimant, the entertaining embodiment of 'vice under character of advantage' in *The Man of Mode* (Chapter IV).

It is true that many of the best modern poets, dramatists, and artists have chosen to adopt a moralistic, condescending attitude towards their subject-matter, and it is hardly surprising that good modern critics are prone to do so too. For instance, T. S. Eliot's influential poem cast a cold eye on J. Alfred Prufrock, and his influential essay on 'Shakespeare and the Stoicism of Seneca' cast an equally detached, severely analytical eye on Hamlet and Othello. According to Eliot, Hamlet, after having 'made a considerable mess of things', dies 'fairly well pleased with himself', while Othello dies *cheering himself up*. Eliot's coolly analytical evaluation of these characters made this specific critical perspective very fashionable. In his famous vivisection of Othello in *The Common Pursuit*, 'Diabolic Intellect and the Noble Hero: or The Sentimentalist's Othello', F. R. Leavis approvingly cited Eliot's verdict on the hero, and certainly Eliot and Leavis may claim a historical place as founding fathers of the modern satirical-moralistic school of literary criticism. Certainly over the past forty years a great many critics (whose work may differ markedly in other ways) have adopted essentially the same, severely moralistic attitudes towards characters in seventeenth-century plays. A quick glance at several discussions of *Othello*[7] and *The Duchess of Malfi* can show how the moralistic attitude has hardened into a critical method that frequently imposes unnecessarily rigid restrictions on characters and critics alike.

Writing in 1944, Leo Kirshbaum argued that 'Eliot could have gone much further' in his analysis of Othello's self-delusions. In his discussion of 'The Modern Othello' Mr. Kirshbaum does go further than Eliot, and he concludes his essay with the statement that 'It is not the hero's nobility in Shakespeare's tragedies, but the flaw, the sin or error that all flesh is heir to, that destroys him.'[8] Surely it is true that Shakespeare's tragic characters, being human characters, share some common human frailties. But it is also true that certain characters are shown to suffer precisely because of their exceptional virtues:

> Know you not, master, to some kind of men
> Their graces serve them but as enemies?

[7] In her British Academy lecture on 'The Noble Moor' (1955), Dame Helen Gardner challenged Leavis's interpretation of *Othello*, and so did John Bayley in his fascinating study *The Characters of Love* (London, 1960). But some members of the moralistic school appear to listen only to each other. For instance, an essay of 1963 on 'The Indiscretions of Desdemona' (discussed below) makes no reference to these discussions, either of which would call the assumptions of this essay into question. I should acknowledge my own debt to Dame Helen Gardner's *The Business of Criticism* (Oxford, 1959) throughout this study.

[8] Leo Kirshbaum, 'The Modern Othello', *Journal of English Literary History*, ii (1944), 283–96; reprinted in *A Casebook on Othello*, ed. Leonard Dean (New York, 1961), pp. 156–68.

> No more do yours. Your virtues, gentle master,
> Are sanctified and holy traitors to you.
> O, what a world is this, when what is comely
> Envenoms him that bears it!
>
> (*As You Like It*, II. iii. 10–15)

Throughout *Othello* (for instance) Iago conspicuously sets out to make the graces of his victims 'serve them but as enemies':

> The Moor is of a free and open nature
> That thinks men honest that but seem to be so;
> And will as tenderly be led by th'nose
> As asses are.   (I. iii. 393–5)

> So will I turn her virtue into pitch;
> And out of her own goodness make the net
> That shall enmesh them all.
>
> (II. iii. 349–51)

And thus the tragic destruction of a Shakespearian hero (or heroine) can result from a complicated combination of causes that may include an evil situation around him, as well as his personal virtues and vices. Shakespeare himself apparently felt perfectly free to provide us with any and all of these (and other) causes for tragic destruction; here stressing one, here emphasizing another, there combining them all. Therefore, to conclude that 'it is the flaw, the sin or error' that destroys Shakespeare's tragic heroes is to oversimplify. Furthermore, this conclusion comes perilously close to reducing the lessons taught us by Shakespeare's richly varied group of tragic figures to the same old lesson gasped out by Preston's King Cambises: 'A just reward for my misdeeds my death doth plain declare.'

Still, this idea of poetic justice is morally satisfying, and by 1963 the author of an essay on 'The Indiscretions of Desdemona' could cite critical support for the notion that Desdemona's terrible fate 'was not totally undeserved'. Though it seems unlikely that any sensitive spectator, watching Desdemona being suffocated by a pillow, would think, 'Well, it does serve her right in a way, because she did something mildly indiscreet back in Act One', this critic argues that elsewhere in the play we are encouraged to deplore Desdemona's failure to behave herself according to the precepts of contemporary courtesy books:

> Desdemona has . . . followed her passion rather than her reason and has been carried away by her love to contract a match which both the world of Venice and the Elizabethan audience would recognize as unnatural. So far Desdemona is not the ideal young lady of the precept books, and the audience, especially the male members of it, could here be expected to judge Desdemona harshly. . . . She undoubtedly loves, esteems, and honors Othello, and she does put up with her husband's unpredictable changes of mood with an almost saintly long-suffering. Still, she is wanting in other matters: she entertains Cassio without Othello's permission; she takes interest in 'forraine' affairs; and she does not wholly obey her husband. She likewise lacks two further virtues listed by Iago: humility in respect of her own wishes, and circumspection in behavior.[9]

At the present time it seems that whenever a critic needs some specific historical licence to deplore the vices and follies of characters in the seventeenth-century drama, all he need do is appeal to traditional moral or social codes. Then he can proceed to spell out just how far given characters deviate from these codes; and thus, with quotations from contemporary handbooks, homilies, and proclamations behind him, and with fallible dramatic characters before him, he can lay on the lash at will, certain that the seventeenth century would have cheered him on. For surely no exceptional, unconventional, or idiosyncratic behaviour should be permitted to exist within the best of all possible moral orders. Neither should any excessive passion, whether on the part of characters or on the part of an audience. Like Leavis and Eliot, Lily B. Campbell deplored A. C. Bradley's 'emotional' and 'sentimental' responses to Shakespeare's tragedies, and she went on to condemn Bradley because of his aesthetic admiration for the dangerous passions of Shakespeare's heroes and villains:

> Now admiration is an alien word in the description of the emotional response to the destroying force in a tragic character . . . admiration

---

[9] Margaret Loftus Ranald, 'The Indiscretions of Desdemona', *Shakespeare Quarterly*, xiv (1963), 127–39. Quotations are from pages 128 and 134.

ought not to be part of a moral response to violations of moral law.
. . . Actually it is apparent that Bradley does admire Shakespeare's
villains and heroes alike if their sins or their passions are only great
enough. . . . It is no wonder that trying to orient his characters in such
a moral universe he could only conclude that 'tragedy would not be
tragedy if it were not a painful mystery'.[10]

But if the poetic imagination can take equal delight in an Iago
and an Imogen, so can the imagination of an admirer of poetry.
And Shakespeare's tragedies do, in fact, exhibit the most painful
mysteries of the human condition.

All too frequently the moralistic school of criticism tends to
reject the old-fashioned tragic responses, admiration, pity, and
terror, in favour of analytical castigation. Simultaneously, it
occasionally prefers its own moral idealism to dramatic con-
sistency[11] and truth to human experience. It is at least possible
that, say, the death of Desdemona may serve to remind us that
in tragedy (as in life) no amount of personal goodness can exempt
certain people from terrible suffering, and that occasionally in
tragedy (as in life) death may represent a cruel injustice rather
than a deserved punishment. The death of Desdemona brings to
mind some harsh questions and some harsh truths about the
tragic nature of a world where people of exceptional virtue may
suffer more than their vicious enemies, and where 'what is comely'
may itself envenom those that bear it. Thus, even as an argument
that Desdemona's death 'was not totally undeserved' shields us
from these questions and these truths, it deprives her fate of much
of its tragic significance. So often, when relatively easy moral
interpretations are imposed upon tragic (and human) facts and
mysteries, these solutions seem too smug and too shallow. For

---

[10] *Shakespeare's Tragic Heroes: Slaves of Passion* (New York, 1963), p. 287.
[11] Because the ending of *Measure for Measure* is morally satisfying, Professor
Leavis argues that we should accept it as dramatically justified. Because the
chilling and terrifying Angelo has suffered, we should willingly let him 'marry
a good woman and be happy' (*The Common Pursuit* (London, 1952), p. 172).
But no moral justification for Angelo's future can ever be fully acceptable
because the marriage to Mariana remains far too incongruously at odds with
Angelo's disturbing idiosyncrasies to be dramatically consistent or dramatically
satisfying.

they seem to be solutions imposed from above, but not to be found within either the tragic condition or the human condition, wherein no such easy solutions exist.

In other instances the elaborate moral apparatus which modern criticism has accumulated over the past years seems to have forced sensitive critics to speak what they morally 'ought to say' rather than what they genuinely feel. For example, when Clifford Leech says what he personally feels about the Duchess of Malfi, his words ring true—true to his own response to the play, and true to Webster's conception of the character as realized in a good production of the tragedy. Here is Leech's excellent description of the Duchess:

> The modern spectator will see her, for the most part, as injured innocence, a woman independent enough to disregard her tyrannical brothers' wishes, and to avow her love for Antonio when his lower rank will not allow him to speak first; a woman loyal and affectionate, a responsive companion, a careful mother; a woman not to be broken either by torment or by the approach of death. Seen in this way, the portrait has charm and yet solidity: we can enter fully into the agonies of Act IV because we have grown into the Duchess's friendship, have seen her loving and merry, have seen her directness in the wooing-scene tempered just sufficiently by a touch of shyness.

So far, so good; for if this description of the Duchess might be accused of 'sentimentality', so can Webster's presentation of her. But suddenly, along comes the spectre of the Great Chain of Being, dragging all its arbitrary moral criteria behind it, to blame the Duchess whom the play praises. And Mr. Leech's sincerely expressed pity and admiration for the character are replaced by a series of moralistic afterthoughts and qualifications:

> Yet we must recognise that her wooing and her marriage with Antonio constitute an overturning of a social code: she defies the responsibilities of 'degree', both as a woman in speaking first and as a Duchess in marrying beneath her. . . . Moreover, she was a widow, and in the seventeenth century the woman who re-married did not escape criticism. . . . A re-marriage for state reasons might have been approvable, but her wooing of Antonio has only the excuse of love. . . . There is,

too, an independence of mind, a note of challenge, in the Duchess's references to religion.[12]

Arguing against the way that Leech (and other critics) bring such rigidly conventional criteria to bear on the Duchess, William Empson concludes that while Webster's sources scold the Duchess for marrying beneath her, and while the play gains interest from debates on this topic, there is no doubt which side the author is on: 'The moral of this play, driven home as with the sledge-hammer of Dickens I should have thought, is not that the Duchess was wanton, but that her brothers were sinfully proud.'[13] Certainly, like her brothers, the Duchess herself is wilful and proud. But in contrast to the motives of her brothers, the motives of the Duchess are never cruel or unnatural ones. She does defy convention, and she does tell a series of lies, but only in order to marry the man she genuinely loves and then in order to protect her family. 'Wherefore are you gentle, strong, and valiant?' Shakespeare's Adam asks Orlando, when these noble virtues are going to make him subject to the wrath of a 'humorous Duke' (As You Like It, II. iii. 6–8). The disturbing question that Adam raises would seem to bring us closer to the tragic predicament of the Duchess of Malfi than any efforts to catalogue her defects. And Mr. Leech himself concludes his discussion of the Duchess with the statement that 'only one memory stays fast with us, that of a woman, young, grey-haired, passionate, exhausted, kneeling down to die'. He also concludes that 'we forget that the Duchess has neglected the specialty of rule' (p. 89). But do we? Do we not remain dazzled by her proud defiance of some of the cruel restrictions of 'degree' that have traditionally shackled women? The Duchess herself does not neglect the specialty of rule at all. She wilfully challenges the validity of her brother's right to govern her life. This play is explicitly concerned with 'integrity of life', and the dramatic action shows us that the

[12] Quotations are from Leech's John Webster: A Critical Study (London, 1951), pp. 69, 72, 75.

[13] See William Empson's review of Leech's Webster: The Duchess of Malfi, in Essays in Criticism, xiv (1964); quotations are from this review as reprinted in ohn Webster, ed. G. K. and S. K. Hunter (London, 1969), p. 297.

Duchess's integrity nobly triumphs beyond death. It converts Bosola and thereby brings the Cardinal to his knees. It also brings Ferdinand to exactly the same mad, despairing death that he had planned for her. By the end of the play the whole society falls on its knees before the Duchess. The action of this tragedy thus calls into question and then condemns certain rigid categories of 'degree'. It is modern criticism, and modern criticism only, that turns the play upside down and uses these categories to damn the Duchess.

In fact, the drama itself demonstrates that seventeenth-century playwrights felt perfectly free to bless some very unconventional, passionate, idiosyncratic, perhaps truly moral, perhaps completely immoral, characters with the unanswerable arguments of poetry and truth to human experience. It is true that the 'proper' relations between men and women, between the individual and society, and between God and men are constantly upset in these plays.[14] But it is also true that the very definitions of what are and what are not the proper relations between men and women, between the individual and society, and between God and man are open to question in any age, in any society. So often the seventeenth-century drama seems much braver than some twentieth-century criticism of it; for where the drama challenges conventional social and moral assumptions, certain modern critics tend to swallow them whole. It is rather as if, in the year 2200, scholars analysing some rebellious Russian tragedies written in 1970, wherein characters challenge the rules of Communist political and social orthodoxy and consequently are destroyed by the state, were to conclude, on the basis of all the contemporary Russian literature in support of orthodox behaviour, that these tragedies *must have been* tracts in support of this orthodoxy too. Because, after all, do they not clearly show just what happened to people whose pride or passion led them to deviate from a code of behaviour which was accepted without question by most Russians in the middle of the twentieth century?

[14] Ian Jack argues that in the works of Webster 'the proper relations between the individual and society, between God and Man, are overthrown' and that Webster 'is a decadent' ('The Case of John Webster', *Scrutiny*, xvi (1949), 43).

Similarly, while it may be true that most seventeenth-century English literature does support conventional ideas, it is not necessarily true that all of it does. It might even be argued that some of the greatest characters, in some of the greatest plays, are very frequently the ones that challenge orthodoxy. And it is unfair to these characters, and to these plays, to impose rigidly orthodox interpretations upon their unorthodox dramatic truths. For where the drama gives us specific truths that may set us free from all sorts of dubious generalizations, much modern criticism retreats right back into the nest of generalizations that the plays themselves challenge. Rather like Machiavelli, the seventeenth-century drama frequently confronted unrealistic formulas about the way the world and its inhabitants ought to behave with uncompromisingly truthful evidence of the falsity of such formulas, given the way the world and its wayward inhabitants really do behave. For this reason, moralists throughout the century disapproved of the drama. It took the ingenuity of twentieth-century scholarship to reverse the dramatic process itself, and to argue that the plays themselves judge their characters according to the very same arbitrary moral and social formulas which they frequently defy. And thus the moral stance of one school of modern criticism has deprived many great plays of their uniqueness, and of their claims to truth.

If the drama is going to hold a mirror up to human nature at all, the mirror is bound to reflect—above all—human individuality. And thus it is going to reflect human passion, wickedness, idiosyncrasy, courage, and isolation. It is inevitably going to show that individuals do not always behave according to moral and social generalizations about how they should behave. And sometimes it is going to reflect the fact that rigid social and moral codes may be unrealistic or unfair to specific individuals. There are, for instance, specific dramatic occasions when children are right and their parents are wrong, and when brave women rightly defy the authority of family, Church, and State. There are specific instances when telling a lie represents supreme dramatic virtue. There are times when human vice takes extremely attractive forms and is rewarded rather than punished. All sorts of unorthodox things happen in these plays—things which are peculiar by rigid moral standards, yet conspicuously true to human experience. But some modern critical discussions of these dramatic events sound just as remote and detached from the world in which such things literally do happen as they are from the texts in which these things happen dramatically.

Thus, while the satirical-moralistic approach to the drama may have provided critics with full employment for a while, it nevertheless fails to pass the final tests of either literal or emotional truth to the plays or to the world that they reflect. While its moralistic formulas provided unlimited subjects for critical castigation, the formulas became too simple, too rigid. And when characters as strikingly different as Desdemona, the Duchess of Malfi, and Dorimant (see Chapter IV) get criticized in strikingly similar ways, it seems time to ask if there is not something suspect, if not something downright absurd, going on. It is true that, like absolutely perfect people, dramatic characters who make not a single, solitary error are hard to come by. Indeed, when we do find them we tend to pass on to more interesting characters, since they tend to be just as dull, formulaic, and cloying as Miss Elsie Dinsmore. For if characters are at all interesting and memorable dramatically, at some point even the most virtuous of them is going to do something or other that deviates from some sort of moral, legal, or social code. Otherwise the character could claim no individuality. And when we have come to the point at which discussions of their deficiencies stand in the way of appreciating the tragic (and human) dilemmas faced by a Desdemona or a Duchess of Malfi, then we have reached the absolute dead end of any understanding of genuine dramatic virtue. And the absolute dead end which is imposed on dramatic vice by moralistic criticism is equally ludicrous.

When it deals with dramatic villains, moralistic criticism belabours the morally obvious and overlooks the dramatically obvious: Etherege's Dorimant, divested of his libertine vices, would be as insipid as Young Bellair. For surely the vices of such a character are precisely what make him dramatically interesting. And very frequently competent dramatists steal the thunder from moralists by making the vices of their characters spectacularly evident. Thus it would seem a little redundant to write a long essay (there is one) proving beyond a shadow of a doubt that Dorimant is a libertine who seduces women, offends against Christian and courtly codes of conduct, and manipulates other characters with cool calculation, since all these points are made explicitly, swiftly, and wittily in the first scenes of *The Man of Mode*. In fact, the drama itself frequently permits us to take the vices of certain characters for granted, and thus allows us to enjoy, with aesthetic and emotional appreciation, the intelligence and power which can go hand in hand with dramatic vice. Too often, when we get long discussions of the frailties of attractive dramatic villains, what we are really getting is a restatement of the obvious along with a plea that the characters cease to be dramatic and behave themselves as decorously as the critic who is writing about them. Indeed, asking the question 'what are their faults?' leads us to foregone conclusions about dramatic villains. The conclusions are foregone because they are taken for granted within the plays themselves. Asking how and why certain villains are so dramatically successful might get us somewhere, but as long as we remain trapped by moralistic criteria, all our discussions of dramatic wickedness are going to take us round in a circle and bring us out just exactly where we came in. We will continue to dance in a ring around the prickly pear of triumphantly successful dramatic vice, while the secret of its power remains in the middle, mocking us.

Thus, whether it deals with wicked characters or with virtuous ones, the modern moralistic interpretation of seventeenth-century drama flourishes at too great a distance from, and even in defiance of, the actual responses which individual plays generate in a theatre. A very powerful scholarly device for getting us to deny our actual responses to certain plays is to imply that these responses are discreditable because they are 'modern', and to argue that a 'contemporary audience' in the early seventeenth century would surely have reacted very differently. Of course we know very little about what Elizabethan and Jacobean audiences were like. But we do know that twentieth-century audiences differ remarkably, from balcony to orchestra, from first night to matinée, from performance to performance, from spectator A to spectator Z. Probably Elizabethan audiences differed too; certainly there is no reason to suppose that they did not. But because our knowledge of them is so nebulous, Elizabethan and Jacobean spectators are wonderfully plastic in the hands of modern critics. They can become whatever the needs of the present argument wish them to become, and they can respond to an individual play in whatever way the present critic wishes them to respond.

The imposition of modern critical responses upon an imaginary 'Jacobean audience' can be illustrated by various twentieth-century appeals to the audience that was present at the opening night of *Measure for Measure*. And surely there is something inherently suspect about these pleas for the support of a spectral audience which is so notably unlike any other collection of individuals ever assembled together, on land or sea, before or since, to watch a play. Reading over the criticism of *Measure for Measure* one may find 'the original audience' transformed (by W. W. Lawrence) into a collection of churlish louts, caring nothing about the legal, social, and moral dilemmas so powerfully presented before them in the opening scenes, but continually panting, thirsting, and lusting for some kind—any kind—of happy ending:

> The audience were interested in the Duke's reforms only in so far as these served the plot. They did not care a straw about the triumph of his theories as a reformer or the moral welfare of Vienna. What they did wish was that the play should end, as a comedy should, in a general atmosphere of happiness.[15]

How does he know? And if Shakespeare's audience would be perfectly satisfied by the dramatic refinements of *Gammer Gurton's Needle*, why did Shakespeare plague them (and us) with worrisome legal, social, and moral issues in the first place? This argument, in fact, serves to get us far, far away from the real responses that *Measure for Measure* has actually provoked, has historically provoked in all sorts of people from Dr. Johnson and Coleridge to R. W. Chambers and E. K. Chambers. These recorded responses

---

[15] W. W. Lawrence, *Shakespeare's Problem Comedies* (New York, 1931), pp. 104–5. For a criticism of this view see A. P. Rossiter, *Angel with Horns* (London, 1961), pp. 111–12.

vary too. And surely there are numerous ways of playing *Measure for Measure* more or less seriously, more or less gaily, with different tonalities and effects. But there should be a limit to how much any critic can use unverifiable evidence about how the 'original audience' might have responded to deny our own right to respond, fully and naturally, to the play itself.

Still reading over the criticism of *Measure for Measure* one suddenly comes across a very different Renaissance man to whom this play is supposed to appeal. He is a solemn, pious cleric, learned 'in the grammatical tradition stemming from Sts. Augustine and Bonaventura', finding the immediate sense of nature 'less important than the theological, moral and mystical lessons that it contains', reasoning by 'analogies, conformities, correspondences, and mystical comparisons'.[16] To justify an interpretation of *Measure for Measure* as an allegory of the Atonement, Roy W. Battenhouse summons forth his very own Renaissance counterpart. And in doing so, he clearly reflects a genuinely modern affection for the abstract, the theological, the symbolic, the allegorical; an affection which frequently exalts Shakespeare's inconsistently portrayed Duke of Vienna into a Symbol of Power Divine, an Ideal Ruler, a More-Than-Prospero who is beyond all mortal and moral categories of judgement. Conveniently, this interpretation of the Duke leaves Mr. Battenhouse free to rail against the moral and mortal frailties of the more interesting characters in the play, Angelo, Isabella, and Claudio. In a peculiar critical inversion, the play's least successfully realized characters, the Duke and Mariana, get critical hosannas, while its most successfully realized characters, the Angelo, Claudio, and Isabella of the first acts, get severe castigation. Similarly, making virtue of the play's necessity, of its happy ending, necessarily involves sacrificing the power of its great opening scenes in order to justify its trite conclusion. However, we may freely choose between these views of the play and of its original audience. For though they are extreme views, they are quite respectable today. And while the 'satirical', the 'theological', and the 'original audience'

---

[16] Roy W. Battenhouse, '*Measure for Measure* and Christian Doctrine of the Atonement', *PMLA*, lxi (1946), 1043.

eras of literary criticism appear to be on the wane, we are still very much in them. The theological perspective on *Measure for Measure* is currently a widely accepted one.[17] Influential recent discussions of their religious imagery and the moral deficiencies of their heroes are trying their best to clamp a solemn theological respectability on to two gaily profane Restoration comedies, *The Man of Mode* and *Love for Love* (Chapter V). Even Congreve's brilliantly incisive comic analysis of 'the way of the world' has been transformed by the modern vogue for abstractions into a monument to a dead idea—into a 'beautifully carved' image of 'a Providential justice which governs all human affairs' (Chapter V). But surely such interpretations reduce rather than reflect the genuine accomplishments of the playwrights. And here perhaps the history of literary criticism itself may be summoned to provide some useful checks and balances against any such limited perspectives imposed upon a play, its author, and its audience.

The main thing, the crucial thing, that the whole body of criticism of Elizabethan and Restoration drama can provide us with is the detailed record of responses to individual plays and to the drama in general by intelligent and sensitive spectators over at least three centuries. And thus it provides us with a clear record of what 'an audience' (which is not only a real one, but very close to an ideal one) truly has wanted from and found in Elizabethan and Restoration plays. Any audience, however homogeneous it might appear to be, is inevitably a collection of very diverse individuals; and the history of literary criticism gives us a collection of individuals who are appropriately different from each other, but who also form an ideally intelligent and perceptive group. And if, say, the ending of *Measure for Measure* has disturbed and disappointed the overwhelming majority of commentators, of all types and schools—including Dr. Johnson and Coleridge, A. C. Bradley and L. C. Knights, E. M. W. Tillyard and Mary Lascelles—in the eighteenth, nineteenth, and twentieth centuries alike, the odds are pretty good that it disturbed and disappointed some of its Elizabethan spectators as well. Even if not, even if the

[17] See S. Nagarajan's Introduction to the Signet *Measure for Measure* (New York, 1964), p. xxii.

ghost of King James himself came back to announce publicly that the original audience viewed *Measure for Measure* 'from beginning to end', as 'pure comedy, based on absurdity, like *The Mikado*, full of topical allusions to a current best seller, and every situation exaggerated into patent theatricality',[18] the recorded evidence of the more complicated response of the critical audience since then would still outweigh this statement because the original audience is dead as earth, but the audience provided by literary criticism survives. And perhaps it is the fittest to survive after all. Very likely it is even more diverse, more sensitive, and more intelligent than the very flower of the Elizabethan theatre-going public could have been, since it includes some of the very greatest English poets and dramatists over three centuries, along with an equally distinguished group of scholars. And whatever the response of the original audience may have been, the series of troubled responses evoked by the play ever since the opening night simply must be taken into account.

For, again, the drama is by its nature a public medium, and though there may be a great many things in a play which do not reveal themselves at a first hearing or even a second, there are certain primary effects which do so reveal themselves. And the accumulated experience of intelligent audiences and readers really represents the best judgement of what these primary effects are. In spite of the fact that they may very well fail to take into account subtleties later discovered by individual critics, the recorded responses of audiences and readers over the years provide us with the best evidence of a given play's overt emotional and intellectual impact. It is precisely because the impact of a particular play was exciting, amusing, disturbing, or otherwise important to actual people in theatres and studies that the play survives and is still read and reacted to, as opposed to the hundreds of thousands of plays that have been forgotten. Thus, something which is not ultimately subject to question has already been decided about any major Elizabethan or Restoration play by the time it reaches a modern commentator. And while the critic who argues that

[18] Josephine Waters Bennett, *Measure for Measure as Royal Entertainment* (New York, 1966), p. 158.

the original audience must have interpreted *Measure for Measure* as a hilarious farce may have a logically coherent position, this critic is not reading the same play that has already been judged to be a very disturbing one by the vast majority of its readers over all these years. Instead of the actual play, this critic gives us a product of the creative and historical imagination of a twentieth-century scholar. But this possible, imaginary *Measure for Measure* cannot survive the test of truth put to it by the actual play, by the real *Measure for Measure*, which has created and does still create serious emotional and intellectual problems for a very large number of extremely sensitive and intelligent readers.

Thus the audience provided by literary criticism may help us to raise (though not fully to answer) the questions: How do we see what is in a seventeenth-century play without imposing on it qualities that are alien to its true nature? When do the imaginative constructions of modern criticism and scholarship (such as ideal moral visions of what characters should be like, ideal notions about what the contemporary audience might have been like, or even ideal theological and historical constructions about what the world might be like) actually blind us to the truths about human experience, to the truths about the way of the world it-self, which are so vividly portrayed within individual plays? Significantly, the plays themselves very frequently confront us with related questions: In what ways do the green worlds of the theatre compare to, differ from, and comment upon the real world of the audience at *A Midsummer Night's Dream* or *The Tempest*? How far can the human imagination go before it tragically or ridiculously divorces itself from empirical reality and from the facts of human experience in *Dr. Faustus* or *The Alchemist*? On the other hand, how far can the human imagination go towards an ultimate assimilation, comprehension, and control of the realities of human experience (*The Tempest*)? And by allowing us in the audience to confront and comprehend the facts of human experience, how far can the imagination of a play-wright go towards showing us how to endure (and thus accept) the tragic realities of *King Lear*, or how to smile at (and thus accept) the social realities of *The Way of the World*?

Indeed, to turn back from critical points of view to dramatic perspectives themselves is particularly refreshing here, where the first plays to be discussed give us clear perspectives concerning the power and the limits of the human imagination. All the subsequent essays are concerned with the imaginative range of individual plays: with the clashing imaginative realms of *Measure for Measure*; with the deliberately restricted focus of *The Man of Mode*; with the deliberately complicated focus of *The Way of the World*; and with the ultimate confrontation with the human condition in *King Lear*. So the best place to begin is with some plays which, in tragic and comic contexts alike, focus on the imaginative range of dramatic illusion itself.

2 'See here my show': theatrical illusions and realities in *The Spanish Tragedy*, *A Midsummer Night's Dream*, and *The Tempest*

'Can you command people's emotions so easily?'
He smiled: 'When you know the plot.'

JOHN FOWLES, The Magus

'ALL shall be well,' says Puck. 'All things shall be peace,' says Oberon. 'There's no harm done,' says Prospero. And thus, through the lines of these supernaturally powerful dramatic spokesmen, Shakespeare himself promises us that no serious harm will come to any of the characters enchanted by his midsummer magic or shipwrecked by his tempest. Similarly, when Oberon and Prospero discuss the magical arts with which they govern their dramatic domains, they inevitably call our attention to the powers and purposes of the dramatist who, in turn, governs them. More than in any other plays by Shakespeare, we view the action of *A Midsummer Night's Dream* and *The Tempest* from the perspective of the playwright. Through Puck, Oberon, and Prospero, Shakespeare informs us how to think and what to think about the characters and events under their supervision. Throughout these plays, Puck, Oberon, and Prospero frequently tell us what is going to happen, or why it is happening, or how it all happened. Indeed, Shakespeare himself seems to have organized these particular comedies in order to examine, while he spectacularly exhibits, the essential nature of his own 'so potent art'. For his dominating concern in both plays (the conceptual Prospero which governs their method and meaning, and to which everything else in them is subordinate) is Shakespeare's own fascination with the nature of dramatic illusion itself; his own pervasive concern with its power, with its limits, and with the various kinds of truth which dramatic illusion may reveal or reflect.

Shakespeare thus crowds both these comedies with references to the drama. There are shows within shows and audiences watch audiences, while Oberon and Prospero, the dramatic embodiments of the playwright's art, bring about the proper solution to the problems of the characters under their supervision.[1] And like so much else in these plays, their concern with the nature of the theatre itself seems characteristically Shakespearian. There is, however, an interesting precedent (though not necessarily a direct source) for the dramatic organization and emphasis which are characteristic of these comedies. In Kyd's *Spanish Tragedy* supernatural overseers predict the outcome of the action and tell us what to think about the characters; multiple audiences watch a play within the play; and the action itself reflects cosmic, human, and theatrical levels of truth. In fact, Kyd's tragedy is the best introduction to Shakespeare's comedies provided by the Elizabethan drama.[2] The comparatively crude *Spanish Tragedy* may have introduced on the English stage the multiple levels of dramatic action and the multiple perspectives on dramatic action which Shakespeare explores throughout his career, perhaps most delightfully in *A Midsummer Night's Dream*, and perhaps most profoundly in *The Tempest*.

Throughout *The Spanish Tragedy*, and very obviously in its climax, Kyd openly calls attention to the conventions of his theatre in order to illustrate the various dimensions of reality that theatrical illusions may reflect. In short, he does exactly the same

[1] My discussion of dramatic illusion is indebted to Leslie A. Fiedler, 'The Defense of the Illusion and the Creation of Myth', *English Institute Essays, 1948*, ed. D. A. Robertson, Jr. (New York, 1949), pp. 74–94; Robert M. Adams, '*Trompe l'Œil* in Shakespeare and Keats', *Strains of Discord* (Ithaca, N.Y., 1958), pp. 52–61; Frank Kermode, *Shakespeare: The Final Plays* (London, 1963); Anne Righter, *Shakespeare and the Idea of the Play* (London, 1962); and David P. Young, *Something of Great Constancy* (New Haven, Conn., 1966).

[2] The importance of *The Spanish Tragedy* to *Titus Andronicus* and *Hamlet* has long been recognized. For discussion of *The Spanish Tragedy* and the revenge tradition see F. T. Bowers, *Elizabethan Revenge Tragedy: 1587–1642* (Princeton, N.J., 1940), pp. 65–85, and Dame Helen Gardner, *The Business of Criticism* (Oxford, 1959), pp. 25–51.

thing that Shakespeare will do with theatrical conventions within the comic contexts of *A Midsummer Night's Dream* and *The Tempest*. A performance of Kyd's tragedy, like a performance of Shakespeare's comedies, involves three groups of spectators (super-human spectators, human spectators on the stage, the Elizabethan audience), and in all three plays individual characters are the authors or directors of various kinds of shows. These intersecting levels of theatricality converge in Kyd's play when Hieronimo, speaking a kind of epilogue to his fatal *Soliman and Perseda*, asks 'How can you brook our play's catastrophe?' (IV. iv. 121).[3] His question is directed to the royal Spanish and Portuguese audience, but his 'play's catastrophe' pleases the soul of Andrea, a super-natural observer (IV. v. 12), and satisfies the audience at *The Spanish Tragedy* itself, an audience which has been coached throughout the action to anticipate revenge, first for Andrea, then for Horatio. Hieronimo's line also calls attention to his role as playwright within the play and to the fusion of dramatic illusion and reality in the catastrophe of *Soliman and Perseda*, and thus it shatters the traditional distinctions between human actions and theatrical imitations of them. Initially, the Spanish and Portuguese audience brings to *Soliman and Perseda* the same assumptions about theatrical illusion that a member of Kyd's audience would bring to *The Spanish Tragedy* itself. The nobles take it for granted that the actors are feigning. They recognize Balthazar in the costume of Soliman, compliment Bel-Imperia on her good acting, and logically assume that the actors will survive the tragic ending of Hieronimo's theatrical entertainment and rise to acknowledge their applause (IV. iv. 20–4). Kyd gives us an account of these assumptions in the very speech by Hieronimo which shatters them:

> Haply you think, but bootless are your thoughts,
> That this is fabulously counterfeit,
> And that we do as all tragedians do:
> To die today, for fashioning our scene,
> The death of Ajax, or some Roman peer,

---

[3] Quotations are from *The Spanish Tragedy*, ed. Philip Edwards (London, 1959).

> And in a minute starting up again,
> Revive to please tomorrow's audience.
>
> (iv. iv. 76–82)

All their previous conceptions about the theatrical situation instantly crumble when the spectators realize that the show they thought was 'fabulously counterfeit' is in fact deadly reality—the human tragedy itself rather than a dramatic imitation of a tragic action. Thus the Spanish and Portuguese audience ceases to experience the aesthetic delight of watching a well-acted play, and experiences the personal horror of death at first hand. And while the members of Kyd's audience view everything that happens on the stage as part of the fabulously counterfeit *Spanish Tragedy*, the action of his play forces them to ask how they might feel if the events seen on the stage suddenly turned out to be real. What if we knew that the actors would not survive their tragic roles?

Then, in the last lines of *The Spanish Tragedy*, Kyd extends his examination of tragic possibilities still further to reveal that when the human tragedy ends, death is only the beginning of an 'endless tragedy' for his villains. To emphasize connections between the eternal and temporal tragedies, between the past, present, and future of his characters, between the beginning and end of his own play,[4] Kyd establishes close rhetorical parallels between Revenge's first speech and his last. The end of his first speech,

> *Here* sit we *down* to see the mystery,
> And serve for Chorus in this *tragedy*,
>
> (i. i. 90–1, emphasis mine)

---

[4] Three levels of time intersect within *The Spanish Tragedy*. First there is the time covered by the action, the time it takes Andrea to see the revenge he desires accomplished. Then there are references to the proper 'season' for action: 'Thou talk'st of harvest when the corn is green . . . The sickle comes not till the corn be ripe.' Finally, there is timeless eternity, the realm of Revenge and of the 'endless tragedy' which begins as Kyd's temporal tragedy ends. Kyd carefully contrasts Revenge, who has no concern for time and urges patience, with Andrea's ghost, who is bound to the temporal world by his memory and by his anticipation of revenge. Thus Andrea provides Kyd with a convenient dramatic metaphor for the continuing pressure of the past on the present, and thus, throughout the play, Kyd extends the ramifications of the action backwards and forwards in time.

is echoed and extended in Revenge's epilogue to Kyd's play:

> Then haste we *down* to meet thy friends and foes,
> To place thy friends in ease, the rest in woes:
> For *here* though death hath *end* their misery,
> I'll *there begin* their *endless tragedy*.
>
>   (IV. v. 45–8, emphasis mine)

Both speeches introduce tragedies, and Kyd's conspicuous word play on 'down', 'here', 'there', 'end', 'begin', and 'endless', contrasts the completed action on the stage to a future where the show goes on for ever, even as it simultaneously combines these two visions. Thus Kyd distinguishes between theatrical tragedy that only seems to end in death, the human tragedy that does end in death, and the endless tragedy that may begin at death. But yet again Kyd makes distinctions in order to break them down. Within his formal framework, the cosmic tragedy contains the human tragedy, which in turn contains the experience of theatrical tragedy. All these tragic realms involve the same actors and the same audiences, while the action and outcome of one is dependent on the action of the others. As we shall see, the same mutual dependence between various levels of reality is stressed by Shakespeare in *The Tempest*, while earlier in his career the supernatural overseers, multiple levels of action, and multiple audiences are transmuted by Shakespeare's art into the pure comic gold of *A Midsummer Night's Dream*.

In *A Midsummer Night's Dream* Shakespeare takes for granted the theatrical elements we saw in *The Spanish Tragedy* and blithely uses them to analyse the essentially absurd, though simultaneously meaningful, nature of all dramatic form, including his own. This analysis of dramatic conventions shapes the form and meaning of the comedy: in the course of it Shakespeare himself questions the validity of every level of reality he so brilliantly creates. Quite casually, he undercuts the existence of his own imaginative scene and characters. A character from a (literally) antique fable, who is performing in Shakespeare's fairy toy, says that he cannot possibly believe 'These antique fables, nor these fairy toys' (v. i. 2–3). Theseus flatly says he does not believe in fairies; but do we really believe in Theseus? Within the action of the play he is no more (or less) real than Oberon, King of Shadows. Shakespeare's comic scene itself dissolves in a similar fashion when, after having poetically convinced us that the stage is a green forest near Athens, Shakespeare brings into this 'green plot' a set of louts who declare they will use the place as a stage. They point in the direction of a tiring-room, which we might otherwise have taken for a 'hawthorn-brake' and decide that it will adequately serve them as a tiring-house (III. i. 2–6). Then the same rude mechanicals go on to make all the wrong assumptions about the nature of theatrical illusions. But what, their play asks, are the right assumptions about theatrical illusions? How does one bring moonlight into a Duke's banqueting chamber or on to the sunlit stage of the Globe? The mechanicals themselves decide that the almanac is useless, and their play later demonstrates that a character signifying Moonshine will not work except for comic purposes. Does Shakespeare's poetry succeed? Yes and no. It ensures that we will accept moonshine imaginatively, but it never suggests that we literally believe in its presence. Thus, even as Shakespeare's play imaginatively 'finds out Moonshine', Bottom and company remind us that it is literally impossible to do so.[5] Equally clearly, nobody literally believes that an actor who appears to be dead really is dead. As *The Spanish Tragedy* reminded us, actors who appear to be stabbed or slain by lions customarily rise to please tomorrow's audience. Then why is it so funny when Bottom, playing the stabbed Pyramus, jumps up to talk back to the Duke? And since we know all along that actors are only actors, why is it so funny when Bottom overhears and replies to comments made by the Athenian audience? The answer to these questions is obvious enough. For comic effects, Shakespeare takes all the dramatic assumptions of his audience and violates them in surprising ways; here exhibiting the power of the imagination, there exposing its absurdities.

Whenever the Athenian audience, or his own, willingly suspends disbelief, Shakespeare points out the utter absurdity of this

[5] 'Now, for the poet, he nothing affirmeth and therefore never lieth,' says Sidney in his *Defense of Poesy*. In *A Midsummer Night's Dream* Shakespeare explores both the truth and the absurdity of this idea.

suspension. Just when we have imaginatively accepted his green plot, we are rudely reminded that it is only a stage. On the other hand, if his own audience, like Hippolyta, is unwilling to suspend disbelief because the action is so silly, Shakespeare points out that from a literal point of view the whole theatrical situation is equally silly, since no play, whether it is good, bad, or indifferent, is more than an illusion: 'The best in this kind are but shadows; and the worst are no worse' (v. i. 210–11). 'Shadows' is an important word in this play. Oberon, who is a kind of dramatic metaphor for the playwright himself, is King of Shadows. The best plays are but shadows. And if any of Shakespeare's shadows have offended, his audience is perfectly free to dismiss his comic masterpiece just as it would dismiss an idle dream (v. i. 412–15). Nevertheless, the Athenian lovers thought they idly dreamed in the forest, but Hippolyta and Shakespeare's audience know that they were permanently affected by the strange happenings there (v. i. 23–7). Metaphorically, then, Shakespeare implies that the drama has the same reality as a dream, the reality of an imaginative experience, no more, no less. If the poet's imagination and the audience's imagination co-operate they will fuse to create the dramatic experience (v. i. 210–11). But at the same time that Shakespeare presents this thesis he attacks it, since he overlooks no opportunity to shatter the very imaginative co-operation he goes to such lengths to create. At every point his imaginative truths clash with equally valid literal truths. The confrontation between these opposing forces is embodied on the stage when Titania woos Bottom with fairy favours while, literal ass that he is, he would much prefer to have his ears scratched (IV. i. 1–27). Thus Shakespeare brilliantly jars factual and imaginative truths and points of view, and proceeds to make comic concord of their discords. He offers no sure victory for either side. The green forest was merely and always a stage, but the vision Bottom could not expound was real.

Like the man who goes about to expound Bottom's dream, the critic who goes about to explain *A Midsummer Night's Dream* volunteers for asses' ears, and Shakespeare says so. The folly of the 'human mortals' in this play is never more conspicuous than when they attempt to criticize, analyse, or even to defend the nature of the drama. The same Athenians we saw unwittingly perform comic dances directed by the amused and patronizing fairies complacently patronize the unwittingly comic performance of the rude mechanicals, who, in turn, are never aware that they are making complete fools of themselves. To turn the screw still tighter, Shakespeare gives to the Athenians the same critical attitudes towards *Pyramus and Thisbe* that might be directed at his own play. Like the ending of *Soliman and Perseda*, *Pyramus and Thisbe* questions the nature of the play in which it appears. 'This is the silliest stuff that ever I heard' (v. i. 209) and 'it is nothing, nothing in the world' (v. i. 78) are lines directed at a dual context. They apply to the terribly wonderful, merry, and tragical theatrical discords of *Pyramus and Thisbe*, and, simultaneously, they apply to the comic masterpiece which contains it, and them. All the clashing perspectives combine to create the comic harmony of *A Midsummer Night's Dream*. It is by the show, the whole show, and nothing but the show, and certainly not by any one attitude expressed within it, that we shall know all that we are like to know about its meaning. No single truth about dramatic illusion makes all things plain in Shakespeare's comedy which, like and by way of the dramatic fiasco and clashing perspectives it contains, deliberately leaves us to 'wonder on'. Ironically, the only unchallenged, clearly stated, uncontradicted, unequivocal truth in the play is the irrefutable generalization, 'Lord what fools these mortals be!' This generalization applies with equal validity to the Athenian audience at *Pyramus and Thisbe*, to the Elizabethan audience at *A Midsummer Night's Dream*, and to all subsequent commentators on the drama itself. For within this particular dramatic context all our rejections of dramatic illusion, and all our willing acceptance of them, are shown to be separate, but equal, illustrations of our inherent folly. And Puck's generalization brings us back to Shakespeare's treatment of superhuman perspectives on dramatic action.

Superhuman points of view constantly determine our responses to *The Spanish Tragedy*, *A Midsummer Night's Dream*, and *The Tempest* alike. In all three plays, two characters with superhuman

knowledge and power look down and comment upon the actions
of the human characters. And one of these supernatural figures
claims to control the action. Revenge assures us that Andrea
will have the vengeance he so impatiently desires, and thus whets
our appetite for a tragic outcome, while Oberon and Prospero
frequently inform us that no serious harm will come to the
characters under their supervision. Simultaneously, characters who
are neither so powerful nor so omniscient create various degrees
of suspense concerning the future action. Andrea's ghost, Puck,
Ariel, and Caliban alike nag, doubt, create difficulties, rebel, or
otherwise question the outcome of the events predicted by their
masters. The conflicts between these superhuman figures allow
Shakespeare and Kyd to combine various degrees of suspense with
various degrees of foreknowledge on the part of the audience.
Kyd's audience, for instance, shares Revenge's knowledge that
vengeance will come, but it also shares Andrea's uncertainty as to
exactly how and when it will come. Also, of course, the omniscience of Revenge, Oberon, and Prospero permits various kinds
of tragic and comic irony, since the 'human mortals' in these plays
have no idea that they are fulfilling tragic or comic patterns, the
outcomes of which are known to their creators, their supernatural
observers, and their audiences. The assumed free will of the characters thus can operate against a dramatic back-drop of supernatural supervision, fixed fate, and foreknowledge absolute, and
the ironic results can be hilarious, tragic, or poignant, or whatever
the playwright desires. In this connection it is illuminating to contrast the differing degrees of supernatural intervention dictated by
tragic and comic forms.

In tragedy, Shakespeare follows Kyd and avoids overt supernatural manipulation of the characters and action. Perhaps the
tragedies by these playwrights reflect contemporary religious
theories which combined an emphasis on divine foreknowledge
with an equal emphasis on the absolute free will and responsibility
of men. In our comedies, however, Shakespeare's superhuman
overseers intervene everywhere, and their intervention is superbly
satisfying. Knowing that benevolent supervisors control everything, we in the audience need never worry about the confusions

on stage. We can safely laugh at them and at the follies and pretensions of the ordinary characters. Such direct control of the action would alter the nature of *The Spanish Tragedy* or *Hamlet*. For Revenge or Andrea to intervene to such a degree in Kyd's play, or for the Ghost to intervene so fully in *Hamlet*, would deprive Hieronimo and Hamlet of the tragic responsibility which they themselves freely accept, and thus would totally change the meaning of their suffering. Like Kyd's Revenge, Shakespeare's witches predict the course of events in *Macbeth*, but they do nothing else to bring it about. And like Andrea, the ghost of Hamlet's father cries out for revenge and shows impatience, but he never intrudes on Hamlet's tragic responsibility. The choices and sufferings of these tragic heroes remain their own, since for Kyd and Shakespeare the very position of tragic hero appears to require an unequivocal acceptance of tragic responsibility and suffering. Thus the degree of supernatural intervention formally differs in these comedies and tragedies, though the function of supernatural figures in terms of dramatic meaning is the same in both genres. In comedy and tragedy alike, they extend the meaning and dimension of the action to symbolic proportions.

On a symbolic level of interpretation, supernatural figures serve as dramatic metaphors for the over-all course of action.[6] Revenge not only predicts, he embodies on the stage, the patterns of retribution which govern Kyd's tragedy. Puck, acting as Blind Cupid, reflects the arbitrary and irrational actions of love-in-idleness. Oberon and Prospero claim the ultimate magical-imaginative power of a playwright who can assure the audience of a happy ending. Ariel and Caliban seem to embody mysterious and powerful forces of art and brute nature which must continually be controlled by the playwright-magician if he is successfully to bring about his happy ending. And in all three plays, power struggles develop between the supernatural teams. Andrea nags Revenge and demands action before the time is ripe. Without the benevolent supervision of Oberon, Puck would wreak

---

[6] For a discussion of supernatural figures as dramatic metaphors for the inevitable course of tragic events see H. D. F. Kitto, *Form and Meaning in Drama* (New York, 1960).

comic havoc, not only without regret, but with pleasure. Ariel wants freedom from Prospero, and Caliban tries to seize it. In an interesting way, these characters and their human counterparts who try to change or speed the course of action attempt to usurp the position of the playwright, to transform themselves from characters into authors. This is, of course, what several characters in our plays frankly admit they want to do. Kyd's Balthazar is described as the 'author' of Andrea's death, which causes Andrea to desire to be the author of Balthazar's death. Hieronimo calls attention to his dual role as 'Author and actor in this tragedy' (IV. iv. 147), and in the fifth addition to the play he goes on to 'applaud' what he has just 'acted' (l. 46). In this connection, Shakespeare's Hamlet and Claudius are similar to Kyd's Andrea, Hieronimo, and Lorenzo, since all these characters urgently try to control the time, place, and course of action and thus, overtly or subtly, aspire to the prerogatives of the playwrights themselves. Perhaps the fact that in his most successful plays Shakespeare gives absolute control of the action only to superhuman characters[7] suggests an ultimate identification between the playwright and God. Certainly Hamlet, Claudius, Hieronimo, Andrea, and Lorenzo all learn, in different ways, that they cannot play God or playwright, that they cannot control the actions of others or the consequences of their own actions; that, in the words of *The Spanish Tragedy*, murder cannot be hid, vengeance will come, but mortal man may not appoint the time. Thus Shakespeare's confrontation between his mighty opposites in *Hamlet* seems distantly related to, though far more subtle than, the conflicting desires of Kyd's characters to become the 'author' within their play. But whatever happens in *Hamlet*, characters are metaphorically identified with playwrights in both our comedies. Like Hieronimo, Puck compares himself to an 'auditor' and 'actor too' (III. i. 70–1). He goes on to behave like a comic playwright when he casts Bottom as 'a stranger Pyramus than e'er play'd here' (III. i. 79), and he speaks like one when he concludes that 'those things do

---

[7] The problems created when, in *Measure for Measure*, Shakespeare endows the Duke of Vienna with the omniscience of a Prospero are discussed in the next chapter.

best please me / That befall prepost'rously' (III. ii. 120–1). But the operations of Puck always are subservient to those of Oberon, the more powerful manipulator, while clearly Shakespeare's most profound exploration of the character–author relationship is his treatment of Oberon's counterpart in *The Tempest*, Prospero.

Discussing *The Tempest*, Coleridge pointed out that there is a pronounced identification between the character, Prospero, and his creator, Shakespeare. 'I have often thought', says Coleridge, 'of Shakespeare as the mighty wizard himself introducing . . . [the] fairest pledge of his so potent art.'[8] And surely Coleridge's response is valid. For whatever the relationship between Prospero and Shakespeare-as-Shakespeare may be, there is a clear identification between Prospero and Shakespeare as Artist. Many characters in other plays compare themselves to playwrights and put on shows, but no other character in the drama of this period acts or speaks so much like a playwright as Prospero. The major word associated with him is always 'Art',[9] and Prospero's 'art' is frequently analogous to, and occasionally identical with, the art of his creator. Like Shakespeare, Prospero deals in illusions which he calls forth for the delight or instruction of others; and, again like a playwright, he has a limited time in which to resolve the difficulties of his tragicomic action. In the course of the play he does many things that Shakespeare does. He raises a tempest; delivers the exposition; tells us what to think about the other characters; creates a few harmless complications between Ferdinand and Miranda; oversees Caliban and Ariel; renders powerless the villains; humiliates the clowns; presents a wedding masque; and finally speaks epilogues to his own dramatic production and

---

[8] *Coleridge's Shakespearean Criticism*, ed. T. M. Raysor, vol. i (London, 1930), p. 131.

[9] See Frank Kermode's Introduction to the Arden *Tempest* (New York, 1964), p. xli. As Professor Kermode points out, the word 'Art' is always spelled with the capital in the Folio, a method of indicating that it is a technical usage. It technically and literally refers to the 'Art' of dramatic poetry in Jonson's lines commending Shakespeare to readers of the Folio:

> Yet must I not giue Nature all: Thy Art,
>   My gentle *Shakespeare*, must enioy a part.
> For though the *Poets* matter, Nature be,
>   His Art doth giue the fashion.

then to Shakespeare's. And in his several speeches saying farewell
to the powers of art, Prospero gives us the artist's personal and
multiple perspectives on his own creations and on his own
position. His creations are gorgeous, but insubstantial; within the
imaginative world of his own creation, the artist occupies the
position of an omnipotent god, but when he steps outside it he
is a vulnerable human being, and furthermore he is at the mercy
of his public.[10]

Throughout his speeches about art, Prospero combines an
emphasis on his vast power with an equal emphasis on its illusory
nature. As a dramatic 'god of power' he can exhaust worlds and
then imagine new ones. Natural and supernatural realms are alike
controlled by his art. Significantly, every word of the speech
describing Prospero's 'so potent art' (v. i. 33–56) applies to Shakespeare's own dramatic practices, and perhaps this is why he decided
to give the Ovidian speech to Prospero.[11] For anyone familiar with
Shakespeare's plays is perfectly familiar with the elves, tempests,
and ghosts which his art, like Prospero's, called forth through the

[10] In 'A Consolatory Tale', Isak Dinesen's artist, Charlie, states that the artist
must love his public as himself, since they are so totally dependent upon each
other. When Charlie reads the Book of Job, he sees himself in the place of
the Lord, his public in the place of Job, 'For the Lord in the whirlwind pleads the
defense of the artist, and of the artist only.' Still, the artist is dependent on
the public, for 'Every work of art', Charlie says, 'is both the idealization and
the perversion, the caricature of itself' and the public has the power to make it the
one or the other. When 'with tears of contrition and pride they acclaim it as a
masterpiece, it becomes that masterpiece which I did myself at first see'. But when
they will not look at it at all it does not exist: 'In vain shall I cry to them: "Do
you see nothing there?" They will answer me, quite correctly: "Nothing at all,
yet all that is I see."' Within Shakespeare's play Prospero is the Lord who com-.
mands tempest, characters, and audience alike. Outside it he and the work of art
in which he appears are, like their creator, at the mercy of the public.

[11] If anyone accused Shakespeare of boasting, he could point to his respectable
source, just as Hamlet points to the 'Italian' source of *The Murder of Gonzago* to
avoid any charge of topicality. Shakespeare elsewhere refers to his earlier plays;
obviously in the histories and subtly, I think, in *Hamlet*, when the actor playing the
elderly Polonius says to Burbage playing Hamlet that he 'did enact' Julius Caesar
once and was killed by Brutus (III. ii. 100–1). It seems likely that the same actor did
play Shakespeare's elderly Caesar. Of course Hamlet–Brutus–Burbage later will
stab Polonius–Caesar–actor, so the theatrical in-joke may foreshadow subsequent
events in *Hamlet*. This possibility is attractive, but I will not go to the stake to
defend it.

'all-daring Power of Poetry' which Jonson claimed for the dramatist. At the same time, Prospero's speeches about art stress the
limits of this power; Prospero has no personal illusions about his
dramatic illusions. He admits with complete acceptance the simple
facts that his magic is rough, his pageants are insubstantial, his
most beautiful dramatic illusions are transient. And to emphasize
these ideas, Shakespeare gives Prospero a masque to present within his play, perhaps because the masque is the most gorgeously
spectacular and, at the same time, the most ephemeral of all
dramatic forms. With very rare exceptions, masques were per-
formed once and once only, and their creators could not but
lament the fact that after a few brief hours their glorious creations
were gone as if they had not been:

> Nor was there wanting whatsoeuer might giue to the *furniture*, or
> *complement*; eyther in *riches*, or strangenesse of the *habites*, delicacie of
> *daunces*, magnificence of the *scene*, or diuine rapture of *musique*. Onely
> the enuie was, that it lasted not still, or (now it is past) cannot by
> imagination, much lesse description, be recouered to a part of that
> *spirit* it had in the gliding by.[12]

Ben Jonson's account of the vanished splendours of his masque,
Hymenaei, sums up the magnificence of theatrical art and its
poignantly transitory nature. And Shakespeare gives Prospero's
epilogue to his last work of art the same power and vastly greater
complexity (IV. i. 146–58). Prospero compares the ending of his
lovely, though ephemeral, world of the imagination to the end
of the great world, and then to the end of a little life. The beauty
and vulnerability of all bright creations, from the spectacle of
the universe on down, that will fade away come together when
Prospero shatters any distinctions between art and life, between
God's globe and contemporary theatrical globes (perhaps the
globe of *Hymenaei* and the Globe Theatre). And, like Prospero's
creation, and like Prospero himself, the world and all we mortal
inhabitants of it are, from the long perspective, such stuff as
dreams are made on, ultimately transitory things, dependent for

---

[12] See *Hymenaei* in *Ben Jonson*, ed. Herford and Simpson, vol. vii (Oxford,
1941), p. 229.

our existence upon some form of creator. Yet finally the artist–creator–character, Prospero, stresses his dependence on us. He is at our mercy, and if he raised the winds at the beginning of his play, we must do so at its end.

Stripped of his art, the artist is totally vulnerable to his public. During the two hours' traffic of the stage he reigns supreme, but his reign is all too brief. At the end of the show, the artist's pure images desert him and he is left, in ordinary life, to lie down in Yeats's 'foul rag-and-bone shop of the heart'. Moreover, without the imaginative co-operation of the audience, the images of the playwright are nothing but cheap circus animals, they are very 'weak masters', and his magic is rough indeed. It is made up of make-up, tinsel, false hair, worn costumes, and rattling machines. These are the facts of theatrical life, and in *The Tempest*, as in *A Midsummer Night's Dream*, Shakespeare reminds us of them.

In his early plays (*A Midsummer Night's Dream*, *Richard II*) Shakespeare gives clashing literal and imaginative perspectives to differing, frequently opposed spokesmen, but here he gives both perspectives to Prospero who (like his creator) sees both sides at once. Finally Prospero tells us that the omnipotence and power of a playwright represent a form of bondage to his works and to his public: bondage to the 'bare island' of the stage; bondage to characters who ostensibly are subordinates but whose problems he must resolve; bondage to the plot, which requires the getting of dukedoms, the pardoning of deceivers; and bondage to the dramatic scene itself which he must somehow transform from one place to another, from an enchanted island back to Naples. Throughout *The Tempest* and so many other plays by Shakespeare, characters have aspired to dramatic omnipotence. Prospero is the one character who has it, and in the end he gives it up and calls it bondage:

> Now my charms are all o'erthrown,
> And what strength I have's mine own,
> Which is most faint. Now 'tis true,
> I must be here confin'd by you,
> Or sent to Naples.
>
> (Epilogue, ll. 1–5)

Still speaking in character, Prospero steps out of the imaginative world of the play to ask co-operation from the historical world of the audience. Throughout his play, characters everywhere have been in bondage to Prospero and asked freedom from him. Ariel has been forced to run errands, Caliban has been a slave, Ferdinand has been forced to carry logs. Now these characters have been set free, but Prospero is still bound by his role as Duke of Milan and by his role as playwright-within-the-play:

> Let me not,
> Since I have my dukedom got,
> And pardon'd the deceiver, dwell
> In this bare island by your spell;
> But release me from my bands
> With the help of your good hands.
> Gentle breath of yours my sails
> Must fill, or else my project fails,
> Which was to please.
>
> (ll. 5–13)

Character and author fuse when Prospero asks the audience to send him back into the imaginary story by means of their applause for a playwright who aimed to please. For if Prospero failed to please, so did Shakespeare; and the art and spirits that Prospero mentions in the end of his epilogue are those of his creator, who used them to enchant his audience:

> Now I want
> Spirits to enforce, art to enchant;
> And my ending is despair
> Unless I be reliev'd by prayer,
> Which pierces so that it assaults
> Mercy itself, and frees all faults.
> As you from crimes would pardon'd be,
> Let your indulgence set me free.
>
> (ll. 13–20)

This surely is not just the statement of a professional playwright's need to win and please customers. The verse conveys a need to bless and be blessed. With proud humility, Prospero asks us to do unto them what he and his creator have done unto others—

extended mercy and liberty. Prospero behaved mercifully towards characters who were as vulnerable to his power as he says he is to ours, and echoing the Lord's Prayer, he reminds us of our own need for mercy. Having given his characters and audience such a happy ending, he asks us to give one to him which will save him from despair. There is no reason why Prospero, Duke of Milan, should despair if he failed to please a Jacobean audience; there are lots of reasons why Shakespeare might. Nevertheless, the reciprocal powers and needs described in the Epilogue apply to everybody: characters, playwrights, and audience alike. And we grant Shakespeare the imaginative indulgence he requests. We accept Prospero and his play graciously, not because we are superior to them, but rather because we see ourselves from Prospero's point of view. Shakespeare's strategy here is unity by encompassment. He pushes our imaginations (along with Prospero's, along with his own) outward to encompass both the action on the stage and the reflex vision of ourselves that we get from being included in that action. From the moment we first meet Prospero we are cordially invited to share the artist's point of view and, in the end, to participate in his rarer action of acceptance and mercy. Prospero's epilogue, in short, completes our transformation into his co-magicians. And his epilogue also provides a basis for some further speculation about the reciprocal relationships between playwrights, characters, and audiences which are emphasized in *The Tempest*, *The Spanish Tragedy*, and *A Midsummer Night's Dream*.

When he speaks as playwright, Prospero (like Oberon and Revenge) speaks to us from the superhuman dimension of art, from an imaginative domain wherein the human artist has perfect control over facts and facets of experience which, in ordinary life, necessarily will exert control over him. As artist, Prospero can control the behaviour of others, he can control the consequences of his own actions, he can control the hazards of existence, and he can even control the forces of nature. But when he emphasizes his own humanity, when he says that he is growing old, when he thinks of his grave, when he tells us that his strength is most faint, and when he implores us to save him from despair, Prospero steps down into the realm of uncontrolled and uncontrollable reality inhabited by his own creator and also by the 'human mortals' in our three plays. For when he describes his own weakness, Prospero speaks from the dimension of human experience which is ruled by mortality and passion, and which Prospero inhabits along with shipwrecked courtiers who can hurt and be hurt by each other, young Athenians who feel the pangs of unrequited love, and Spanish and Portuguese nobles who suffer the consequences of their own decisions and the decisions of others. And we who sit in the audience are thus reminded that we ourselves also inhabit, even as we observe, both the superhuman-artistic and the human-mortal dimensions of experience. For while Revenge, Oberon, and Prospero pass on to us the privileged information of a play-wright, whereby (for instance) we know more about Antonio than Alonso knows, more about Demetrius than Helena knows, more about Lorenzo than Hieronimo knows, the action of all three plays reminds us that this total insight into the motives of others is no more available to us in our own everyday lives than it is available to the vulnerable characters on the stage. Indeed, Prospero, Oberon, and Revenge themselves make it clear to us that we know what we know precisely because we are members of an audience who are granted, for the duration of these plays, the insights into their own creations which are possessed by their creators.

Time after time, then, our three plays emphasize the single most obvious, most basic, fact about the drama itself; for they continually stress the fact that the playwright is always in control and therefore (and *only* therefore) everything will work out in an appropriately comic or appropriately tragic way. In *Pyramus and Thisbe*, and elsewhere in *A Midsummer Night's Dream*, Shakespeare reminds us that the course of true love does not usually run as smoothly as it runs in the end of his comedy. Throughout *The Spanish Tragedy* the ghost of Andrea worries that the villains will get off scot-free—and so they might if they had committed their crimes in real life, and not in a tragedy under the direct super-vision of Revenge. And in *The Tempest* Prospero himself makes it impossible for us to share Miranda's unqualified idealism con-cerning the 'brave new world' that lies outside the control of his art. All three plays thus define their tragic and comic dimensions of dramatic art by contrasting their own orderly processes to the disorder of ordinary experience. But all three plays also (and simultaneously) remind us of the essentially arbitrary, amoral, and unjust nature of their own comic and tragic forms.

In the Epilogue to *The Spanish Tragedy* Kyd contrasts the justice of a morally ordered ending with the injustice inherent in his own tragic level of action. As the characters enter his supernatural domain, Revenge assures us that the virtuous ones will find eternal happiness in the Elysian Fields while the villains will suffer eternal punishments in Tartarus. But the just rewards and punishments which are distributed to Kyd's characters in their afterlives contrast pointedly with the injustices which they experienced in their mortal lives, where 'good old Hieronimo' suffered far more than the evil Lorenzo, and where good and evil characters alike finally died together on the tragic stage. Thus Kyd's Epilogue directs our attention to the injustice implicit in his own tragic designs, whereby no amount of virtue on Hieronimo's part could keep the hero from suffering terribly.

Comic form, of course, may be equally amoral and equally unfair to its characters. The conclusion of *The Tempest* gives no special rewards to the virtuous characters, and no special punishments to the vicious ones. Speaking for the playwright himself, Prospero invites the villainous Antonio, as well as the loyal Gonzalo, to join in his circle of comic concord. In fact, in these three plays, and in other great plays as well, the moral virtues and vices of the individual characters have nothing to do with the essential nature of the dramatic destinies imposed upon them by the playwrights. For if Oberon makes certain that Demetrius will wake up at exactly the right time to bring about a happy ending, Shakespeare himself elsewhere makes equally certain that Juliet will wake up at exactly the wrong time and thus ensure an appropriately tragic ending. And so, because of the comic design of *A Midsummer Night's Dream*, the fickle Demetrius lives happily ever after; and because of the tragic design of *Romeo and Juliet*, one of the sweetest ladies in English drama dies before she has lived for sixteen years. Still, the moral inequities of tragic and

comic form alike have a great deal to do with their rightful claims
to be the mirrors of nature itself. For they accurately reflect the
very nature of things which obviously permits good, bad, and
indifferent people to join each other in the dance of life, and then
finally insists that they join each other yet again in the dance of
death. Similarly, when these plays make it evident that the tragic
or comic forms which they impose upon their characters are
unknown and unknowable to the characters themselves, they
accurately mirror the fact that the ultimate purposes of nature
itself remain unknown and unknowable to mortal men.

Thus, it seems exactly right for Jan Kott to quote as a gloss on
The Tempest the following words of Joseph Conrad:

> The ethical view of the universe involves us at last in so many
> cruel and absurd contradictions, where the last vestiges of faith, hope
> and charity, and even of reason itself, seem ready to perish, that I
> have come to suspect that the aim of creation cannot be ethical at all.
> I would fondly believe that its object is purely spectacular: a spectacle
> for awe, love, adoration, or hate, if you like, but in this view—and
> this view alone—never for despair! Those visions, delicious or poignant,
> are a moral end in themselves. The rest is our affair.[13]

For when he speaks as playwright at the end of *The Tempest*
Prospero himself looks down on the spectacle of the whole world,
on friends and enemies alike, with the negative capability of an
artist contemplating his own creation. He can accept Caliban
('this thing of darkness I acknowledge mine') and Miranda alike
as parts of the spectacle. But this divine acceptance, which can
accept the existence of (and allow freedom to) the best and the
worst, the beautiful and the monstrous alike, is not arrived at
without difficulty, even in the green world of the artist's imagination, where the artist himself continually charts our path and we
are effectively distanced from our personal fears and concerns.
Indeed, this attitude conflicts almost to the end with Prospero's
own personal indignation and rage at the evil characters, and he
must struggle to achieve it for himself (and for us):

[13] Joseph Conrad, *A Personal Record*, Ch. V, quoted by Jan Kott in 'Prospero's
Staff', *Shakespeare our Contemporary*, tr. Boleslaw Taborski (London, 1967),
p. 277.

Though with their high wrongs I am struck to th' quick,
Yet with my nobler reason 'gainst my fury
Do I take part; the rarer action is
In virtue than in vengeance . . .

(v. i. 25–8)

As artist, Prospero can accept everything, even his enemies, with a kind of total comprehension; as a passionate human being, who has suffered from treachery, he must struggle to forgive.

An excellent gloss on Prospero's two different attitudes towards his enemies appeared (in a very different context) in an address about human perception which A. H. Maslow delivered to the American Psychological Association. Maslow observes that in certain supreme experiences, whether of love, of aesthetic contemplation, of creative exhilaration, or of intellectual insight, mature people (like Prospero) may relate themselves in a 'divinely impersonal' way to the world, to their own situations, and to all sorts of people whom they would normally condemn and fear: murderers, rapists, exploiters, each other, etc.[14] This mode of perception (in Maslow's terms) is ego-transcending, self-forgetful, desireless, fearless, unselfish, detached, all-forgiving, all-accepting. When people experience it they can and do possess the traditionally godlike attitudes which Shakespeare gives to Prospero, and thus they can contemplate the spectacle of evil as we contemplate wild animals and storms: 'It is in principle possible to admire the beauty of the flood or the tiger in the moment before it kills or even to be amused by it.' Of course it is much harder to achieve this attitude towards human actions that are harmful to us, but it is 'occasionally possible, and the more matured the man is, the more possible it is' (p. 88). In short, this highest mode of human perception is a very aesthetic mode of perception. As such, it may conflict intrinsically with the practical and with the moral reaction to life. It can comprehend an Antonio as easily as a Gonzalo; an Iago as easily as an Imogen; a tiger as easily as

[14] A. H. Maslow, 'Cognition of Being in the Peak Experiences', reprinted in *The Journal of Genetic Psychology*, xciv (1959), 43–66, and in his *Toward a Psychology of Being* (Princeton, N.J., 1962), pp. 67–96—page numbers of the latter work are cited in my text.

a lamb.[15] But these strange heights of acceptance quite literally represent the rarer action of the human spirit. Ordinarily, like Prospero threatened by Caliban and furious with Antonio, or like Hamlet confronting Claudius, we all necessarily must see and respond to the world and to other people in personal, practical, and moral terms. We perceive them primarily in reference to ourselves and our own motives and therefore we have to evaluate, fear, judge, and condemn (p. 77).

Thus, while it is true that all human perception is subjective and individual, there are clear distinctions between our perceptions of external objects as relevant to our personal concerns and as irrelevant to them. Maslow compares these modes of perception to a microscope, 'which can reveal through histological slides either a world of *per se* beauty or else a world of threat, danger, and pathology' (p. 72). The scientist, viewing a cancer through the microscope, may find it a fascinating, awesome, intellectually exciting, intricately designed organism, but if he then learns that the cancer is his own, the personal threat posed will radically alter his vision of the organism revealed by the microscope. Similarly, the Spanish and Portuguese audience aesthetically enjoyed watching the tragic action of *Soliman and Perseda* until the action proved to be of deadly personal relevance. Like Maslow's microscope, the drama itself can focus the vision of its audience either personally or impersonally, or both ways in differing combinations. For instance, an audience observing the villainous Claudius on his knees struggling to pray may find him impersonally fascinating, intellectually exciting, temporarily sympathetic, an intricately designed character worthy of aesthetic

---

[15] See Keats's letter to Richard Woodhouse (27 Oct. 1818) stating that the poetical character 'does no harm from its relish of the dark side of things any more than from its taste for the bright ones; because they both end in speculation'. And of course Prospero finally sets his darker subjects free to go their own ways and to refuse, if they wish, to join his circle. See W. H. Auden's verse fantasia on *The Tempest*, where Shakespeare's silent villain, Antonio, makes this refusal clear:

> Your all is partial, Prospero;
> My will is all my own:
> Your need to love shall never know
> Me: I am I, Antonio,
> By choice myself alone.

admiration. Hamlet, observing Claudius at the same moment, violently, without qualification, resolves to damn him. From Hamlet's point of view, Claudius is the cancer personally threatening him and destroying everything precious in Denmark, and Hamlet's is, of course, the point of view which, almost everywhere else in the play, we in the audience are encouraged to share. Thus certain plays may call for very different kinds of perception and response. Some plays permit us gleefully to enjoy spectacular human vices which in real life would be appalling threats to us. Other plays appeal directly to our emotions and arouse very personal fears and tears. The greatest tragedies surely evoke an intense personal sympathy for human suffering at the same time that they communicate a divinely impersonal acceptance of the human condition. But some modern criticism fails to take these differing dramatic perspectives into account. It gives us detached, intellectual catalogues of the frailties of characters who, on the stage, evoke sheer pity and terror (Othello, Desdemona, the Duchess of Malfi) and then turns around and shows exactly these emotions towards certain characters in *The Man of Mode* who deserve neither of them and are better off without them. The great playwrights, however, usually make the desired responses very obvious.

Looking back on *The Tempest*, it seems obvious that the dramatic focus of the play leads the audience towards a final participation in Prospero's imaginative acceptance of the spectacle of the world, towards the 'negative capability' which Keats attributed to the artist, toward the 'godlike' cognition which Maslow attributes to a few exceptionally mature people and to everybody in the rarer moments of ultimate experience and perception. It seems equally obvious that other plays call for precisely the opposite response. The first half of *Measure for Measure*, for instance, encourages its audience to recognize the cancer under the dramatic microscope as its own; to confront a world of threat, danger, and pathology; to become intellectually entangled in legal and theological pros and cons; to become emotionally involved with the characters, and thus to evaluate, condemn, and judge them, for good or ill, in passionate, personal terms. When therefore, midway through the play, Shakespeare interposes the Duke between us, the other characters, and the action, and thus tries to shift our dramatic focus from an intensely personal point of view to the detached perspective appropriate for his comic ending, he creates problems for his characters and his audience which the critical free-for-all surrounding the play can illustrate, but cannot solve. There is, in fact, no better illustration of the limits which the artist himself sets for literary criticism than Shakespeare's most conspicuously flawed masterpiece; for our clashing personal and impersonal responses to the two parts of *Measure for Measure* are neither reconciled nor encompassed within the imaginative scope of the tragicomedy itself.

3 'They that have power to hurt and will do none': tragic facts and comic fictions in *Measure for Measure*

> We ourselves esteem not of that obedience, or love, or gift, which is of force.   MILTON

I T is an old paradox of literary history that certain works which confront their critics with conspicuous flaws (like *Measure for Measure*) nevertheless remain greater than similar works which pose no serious difficulties (like Marston's *The Malcontent*). Indeed, the simple fact that a play which creates insoluble critical problems can still demand the adjective 'great' (nobody calls *Measure for Measure* 'good') serves as an important reminder of the essentially mysterious nature of literary greatness. The most brilliant critic living cannot tell a gifted young poet how to write a masterpiece any more than our categories of genre can explain why masterpieces so often transcend generic categorization. And *Measure for Measure* still stubbornly defies the whole modern range of critical methods and historical information to solve its problems. There are at least three books on Shakespeare's tragicomedy and there have been discussions galore.[1] But nobody has come up with any over-all interpretation of the play which cannot be refuted or countered by some opposing interpretation with equal, if separate, validity. The play itself splits into parts so essentially different that they compete with each other,[2] and so do our conflicting, mutually contradictory, responses to them.

---

[1] For a good survey (and bibliography) of criticism of this play see Jonathan R. Price, '*Measure for Measure* and the Critics: Towards a New Approach', *Shakespeare Quarterly*, xx (1969), 179–204.

[2] A full account of the stylistic differences between the two halves of the play appears in E. M. W. Tillyard's *Shakespeare's Problem Plays* (London, 1951), pp. 123–38.

The detached point of view predominant in the second half of the play does not extend back to encompass the first half, and the intense personal involvement aroused by the first half is not sustained or even permitted in the second half. In short, the first half of the play has the power to hurt; the second half will do none. The play refuses to do the thing it most did show. The first half moves others (us) to desire tragedy and then the second half asks them (us) to be unmoved, cold, and to temptation slow. Each half thus represents a dramatic country on which the other half has declared war. And there are other problems as well. Maybe a quick account of the way *Measure for Measure* differs from *The Malcontent*—a comparable and very successful tragicomedy—followed by a discussion of key difficulties with *Measure for Measure* can help explain why it remains a great play which haunts the memory and the imagination, and also remains a frustrating, annoying companion, constantly nagging about problems which nobody can solve for it, since they are problems that have no social, theological, or dramatic solution.

It is obvious at a glance that the general tragicomic outlines of *Measure for Measure* and *The Malcontent* are similar, and their similarities can be swiftly, if dully, described. Within the corrupt societies of both plays a disguised duke manipulates characters and intrigues so that the outcome of a play which might otherwise have developed in the pattern of revenge tragedy results in mercy and harmony. Here the similarity ends and some illuminating differences emerge. Where the ending of *Measure for Measure* creates disturbing problems for its audience, the conclusion of *The Malcontent* satisfies its audience, or at least a common reader has no objection to that conclusion. Where Marston's play is all of a piece throughout, the language and action of Shakespeare's play split into two distinct parts. But the most noticeable difference between the two tragicomedies lies in their initially differing modes of characterization.

Marston's characterization poses no problems for his audience. His characters are, every one of them, familiar types on the Elizabethan stage. The disguised Duke Altofronto, speaking as Malevole, sounds enough like Jonson's Macilente and other characters of the same type to be readily accepted as the play's satiric spokesman from the moment he first opens his mouth. Marston's villain, Mendoza, is a nicely portrayed Machiavel with a Marlovian flair for overstatement. The other characters need no more detailed introduction to any audience or reader even superficially familiar with their dramatic predecessors and contemporaries. We have Celso, the loyal friend and confidant; Bilioso, the doddering old man; various licentious courtiers; a fool; a virtuous duchess; a bawd. However bitter Marston's presentation of his upside-down world may be, its inhabitants are our old dramatic friends whose ancestors, siblings, and progeny people many of the most popular plays on the Elizabethan stage. Familiarity, in this instance, breeds relaxed acceptance and enjoyment. We know exactly what to expect from Marston's characters, and they gratify us by living up to our expectations (in the manner of Jonson's 'humour' types). All Marston has to do, given his skilful depiction of these well-known types, is to set them in action in a series of interesting intrigues. And his characters are such conventionally theatrical figures that even when the action moves in an ominous direction, nobody in the audience really worries. The highly theatrical posturing, running about, double murder assignments, and masque are lively, vivid, and fun to watch. Marston's world is certainly out of joint, but from the beginning it is so obviously a theatrically disordered world that there is no surprise when the playwright —via his spokesman and agent, Malevole–Altofronto—manages, theatrically, to set it right. For any problems created by the dramatic intrigues of one set of characters may be effectively solved by the dramatic intrigues of another group of characters, and dramatic 'humours' can be expelled dramatically. Also, the satire is consistently, if savagely, funny. The perfume sprayed on the stage in the opening scene, Malevole's gleeful exposures of everyone, Mendoza's exaggerated, contradictory, speeches about the nature of women, all move the play's satirical thrust in the direction of comedy. Marston further makes it impossible to worry seriously about the fate of his characters because he continually reminds us that Malevole–Altofronto will take over just as soon as time and place adhere. Their predicaments are serious, and the corrupt court of *The Malcontent* evokes righteous indignation from its inhabitants; but Marston rightly calls his play a comedy since, however dark and devious his dramatic world may be, his primary emphasis falls on the dramatic intrigues, and not on the suffering which it causes.[3]

The situations presented in the first half of *Measure for Measure* cause some extreme suffering, and Shakespeare's major characters evoke no laughter. If, in the first half of his play, Shakespeare exaggerates the traits of Angelo and Isabella, he does so in ways significantly different from Marston's stylized exaggeration. Where Marston gives us old dramatic acquaintances, Shakespeare gives us characters different from any of the dramatis personae in his own works or in those of his contemporaries. Where Marston anchors his characters and action in the dramatic tradition, Shakespeare looses our dramatic moorings at the same time that he disturbs familiar ethical and moral assumptions. There are lots of villains like the machiavellian Mendoza—there is none like Angelo. Isabella's concern for her chastity goes far beyond the conventional purity of Marston's Maria (or Whetstone's Cassandra) and becomes the fiery asceticism of a medieval saint. Until Act III, Scene i, line 153 of this play, Angelo, Isabella, and Claudio (when he faces death) have the classical intensity of figures in the *Antigone*. The three are all absolutists. Angelo is absolute for the letter of the law, then for Isabella. Isabella is absolute for chastity. Claudio soon becomes absolute for life. In their great confrontation scenes Shakespeare moves this triumvirate in what seems to be an inexorably tragic direction. Surely an audience which has watched these confrontations is left not with a vague impression but with the absolute conviction that, given their situation, each of these characters would choose to bring tragic suffering upon another.

---

[3] See Marston's Prologue to *The Malcontent*, which reminds the reader of the lively action which his comedy had on the stage. Of course a satiric point of view similar to Marston's governs the action of contemporary tragedies as well as contemporary comedies. The same point of view and a markedly similar cast of characters, appropriately darkened for tragic purposes, appears, for instance, in Tourneur's *Revenger's Tragedy*. In both *The Malcontent* and *The Revenger's Tragedy* the stylized characters and the satirical perspective on them lend aesthetic distance to the action.

Indeed, Angelo, Isabella, and Claudio themselves (in turn) convince us that Angelo would, without doubt, take Isabella and dishonour her in spite of his own horrified conscience; that Isabella would never yield to Angelo, even to save her brother's life; that Claudio could not willingly choose death, even to save his sister's honour. In the first half of the play Shakespeare makes these tragic decisions seem both probable and necessary. Thus, just before he alters the course of action in the direction of comedy, he passes a dramatic point of no return. For he creates in his audience a very simple and passionate appetite to watch these characters enact their tragic choices.

Furthermore, whether we approve or violently disapprove of them, and however they may shock or infuriate us by their personal assumptions and behaviour, Angelo, Claudio, and Isabella force us to experience their dilemmas with them. On a personal and intimate level, which the words of Marco Mincoff both illustrate and describe, the first half of this play gives us 'a man who believes he is more than his fellows, who stumbles and falls, and struggles blindly to understand how he has become the thing he despises'. The true meaning of Angelo, for Mr. Mincoff, may lie in 'the fact that we have experienced his fall with him . . . have felt his very repressions bursting out with double force, and his bewilderment when the staff he has always relied on, his freedom from temptation, collapses under him' and 'that we have felt, even in him, something of the potential splendour of humanity'. It gives us a girl, 'with an ideal of virtue beyond this world', who is faced 'with the necessity of consigning her own brother to death, and turning from him in horror when he sinks to the level of her tempter'. It gives us her brother, 'brought up to regard death as preferable to dishonour and steeling himself to meet it steadfastly, yet breaking down when a hope of life offers itself'. And it shows them to us in a complex set of interactions that form a moving and exciting story. It does not ask us either to accept or to reject the assumptions on which these people believe they must act, it only asks that we should feel with them, and realize how hard it may be to live up to such assumptions. It presents these figures to us in a language so pregnant and splendid that it lends to them an added significance and an added depth, so that they seem both larger and truer than life.'[4] If only half of a play can evoke this kind of response from a perceptive and intelligent critic (and from many others like him), it is surely part of a very great play. But the deeply involved, highly personal nature of this response suggests that this half of *Measure for Measure* is more readily comparable to *Hamlet* than to *The Malcontent* or *The Tempest*.

Throughout *The Malcontent*, the point of view of Malevole–Altofronto, the satirist who exposes and castigates the vices and follies of the other characters, is the predominant one, the one which we in the audience are encouraged to share. Marston's comedy is an imitation of follies and vices which the playwright (in the words of Sidney's *Apology*) 'representeth in the most ridiculous and scornfull sort that may be, so as it is impossible that any beholder can be content to be such a one'. And Marston's stylization of his characters allows us to heap our scorn and ridicule on them from a safe dramatic distance. In *The Tempest* Prospero's perspective (the perspective which dominates the play and which we are encouraged to share) allows us to view the characters and action from a great height, like a god contemplating the theatre of the world without tears or fear. Too frequently, I think, modern criticism takes it for granted that we watch *all* plays and their characters either with the diagnostic, highly critical, moralistic superiority of the satirist, or with the cosmic, philosophical detachment of a Prospero who can control his own emotions as perfectly as he controls the action. Mr. Mincoff's vision of the characters and action of *Measure for Measure* fits neither of these categories. It is very personal, as well as aesthetic; very emotional, as well as rational. He speaks as a human being engaged by the play as well as a critic detached from it. He has been *moved* by Shakespeare's 'hart-ravishing' presentation of 'virtues, vices, and passions so in their natural states, laide to the view' that the spectator, along with the characters and their language, 'may be tuned to the highest key of passion' (Sidney's

---

[4] See the full discussion by Marco Mincoff, '*Measure for Measure*: A Question of Approach', *Shakespeare Studies*, ii (1966), 141–52.

phrases about poetry's power to move its audience). Where *The Malcontent* and *The Tempest*, for their individual and proper dramatic reasons, subordinate their emotional impact for the sake of and by means of other kinds of effects, the first half of *Measure for Measure* makes a direct assault on the emotions. For this reason, Mincoff's response seems to me to be much truer to this part of the play than a critical approach which assumes that we are detached, distant, and uninvolved, unmoved and unchanged by the dramatic experience, and which assumes that our perceptions of the play can only be distorted by our emotions.

D. L. Stevenson, for instance, has argued that the audience, throughout this play, is encouraged to examine the moral decisions and conflicts of the characters with 'a sardonic detachment equal to that of the Duke', and that the characters here are 'deliberately simplified and made less interesting in themselves than is Hamlet, for instance, or Falstaff'.[5] Much of what Mr. Stevenson has to say is perfectly true—of *The Malcontent*. And do we really want to see *Measure for Measure* turned into a duplicate of Marston's play? On the contrary, the history of criticism of *Measure for Measure* reflects just about every possible attitude towards the moral decisions and conflicts of the characters except sardonic detachment. For while it is true that a detached perspective on the characters and action is encouraged by the second half of the play, initially there is no dramatic insulation between our personal responses and characters who arouse in us simultaneous pity and terror and, in the process of doing so, sear themselves into our imaginations. The Duke (who will be discussed later) reveals no firm standpoint remotely comparable to the consistent attitudes provided for us by Malevole and Prospero. There is no traditionally satiric, comic, or romantic stylization of the central characters or their language that effectively lends aesthetic distance. Again, the first half of *Measure for Measure* has the dramatic impact of a play comparable to *Hamlet*.

[5] D. L. Stevenson, *The Achievement of Shakespeare's 'Measure for Measure'* (Ithaca, N.Y., 1966), pp. 12, 14. Mr. Stevenson himself later changes his mind and acknowledges that 'what is held brightly in focus is an excited and intensified sense of the immediate knowableness of a created and complex being: a Hamlet, an Isabella' (p. 120).

Certain great plays may be compared to the remarkable characters they so frequently contain, or to the stars who act in them,
since they are all capable of demanding an indelible and passionate
response from their observers. This capacity is ultimately mysterious, like the appeal of a supremely vivid human personality,
whether it be expressed in the play, *Hamlet*; embodied in its
central character; projected by its star player; or inherent in its
author. Play, character, actor, and playwright all may share the
power to evoke not only an aesthetic, impersonal fascination, but
also to compel a deep, instinctual, highly emotional, and private
response from their observers and in doing so to take on an
independent existence in the observer's imagination. For instance,
characters like Hamlet and Falstaff have had, throughout the
years, personal after-lives in the imaginations of their admirers
that exist quite independently of their original dramatic contexts.
They have somehow transformed themselves from component
human parts in given dramatic spectacles into spectacular human
beings interesting for their own sakes. Earlier criticism, such as
The Fortunes of Falstaff, Coleridge on Hamlet, Bradley's *Shakespearean Tragedy*, bears witness to this phenomenon. Modern
criticism, which frequently argues that such characters have no
right to any existence apart from their immediate dramatic context, tends to imply that this phenomenon does not or should not
exist. But whether or not it should, it does. The passionate
adoration which individual critics accord to their own, private,
saintly, or lovable Isabellas, and the equally passionate revulsion
which other critics express towards their own smug, vixenish,
intolerant, selfish Isabellas, testify to Isabella's after-life in the
heavens or hells assigned to her by individual imaginations.[6] This
phenomenon, as it recurs over time, demonstrates that, like Fal-

[6] For examples of saintly or lovable Isabellas see Roy Battenhouse, 'Measure
for Measure and Christian Doctrine of the Atonement', PMLA, lxi (1946), 1029–
59; R. W. Chambers, 'Measure for Measure', in Man's Unconquerable Mind
(London, 1952), pp. 277–310; Eileen Mackay, 'Measure for Measure', Shakespeare
Quarterly, xiv (1963), 109–13, and others cited by D. L. Stevenson (n. 5, above),
p. 89. For smug, selfish Isabellas see Arthur Quiller-Couch's Introduction to his
edition of the play (Cambridge, 1922), pp. xxix–xxxiii, and U. M. Ellis-Fermor,
The Jacobean Drama (London, 1958), p. 262.

staff, the plays, characters, artists, and individuals who have the mysterious power to move—to delight, to hurt—are the cause of wit in others. They somehow make people see better, know things, feel them intensely, and it does not especially matter (in art) whether the insight communicated is beautiful or terrible, good or evil, disturbing, pleasant, or amusing. It is doubtful if the secret of this power can be rationally explained. There is something irrational and compulsive about any rapt reader or audience. Tolstoy thought that the vogue for Shakespeare was a kind of contrived mass mania, and perhaps this is exactly what certain great plays and characters create—a mass mania, contrived by their creators and admirers, that survives the tests of time and truth posed by the imagination of individual readers. As Dr. Johnson said, a substantial period of time is necessary to establish the enduring validity of a classic writer or work, and in the experience of the individual reader or playgoer the same principle applies. Our personal classics—plays, characters, or writers—are remembered for a lifetime and sought out again and again in different periods of that lifetime. They make it impossible for us to forget them. They will not let us go.

The first half of *Measure for Measure* has these indelible qualities. The characters, their lines, their cruel dilemmas are quite impossible to forget; for Shakespeare forces us along with Angelo, Isabella, and Claudio on their way to 'temptation where prayers cross'. He exhibits before us, with ruthless and disturbing power, the irreconcilable contradictions which very frequently arise, in life itself, between equally valid claims to human devotion. He shows us the contradiction between Isabella's ideal of her own chastity-integrity and the claims of her devotion to her brother; the contradiction between Claudio's will to live and his devotion to his sister; the intrinsic contradictions between the claims of the rule of law, the claims of ideal justice, and the claims of Christian mercy. Here, surely, the truths of literal reality and the artist's imaginative presentation of them are fused, for the sheer power of Shakespeare's dramatic exhibition of these conflicts drives home the harsh but undeniable fact that certain contradictions between equally valid claims to human devotion may be totally irreconcilable.

And the major problem in this 'problem play' is precisely that the memory of the characters, their speeches, and their conflicts between mutually exclusive moral alternatives simply cannot be revoked by the theatrical intriguing of a Duke who argues that measures can always be taken, that solutions can always be found, that 'all difficulties are but easy when they are known'.

It is true that all things are possible in the drama. Shakespeare has a perfect right to change his mode of characterization and the direction of his action in the middle of the play if he wants to. The problem here is that he cannot alter the memory of his own audience. For by the time Shakespeare shifts his dramatic emphasis in the direction of intrigue and comedy, his earlier movement towards tragedy has become part of the spectator's memory, part of his personal experience, part of his own private past. And, in the words of Milton,

> Past who can recall, or done undo?
> Not God Omnipotent, nor Fate!

Not even Shakespeare. For while we can easily be taught something new, we cannot be commanded to forget information which is implanted in our minds by the command itself: 'Try to count to ten without thinking of a rabbit.' The dramatic shock of watching an Angelo previously unmoved and invulnerable to temptation become obsessed by a young novice makes its awesome dramatic impact before Mariana's name is ever mentioned. The subsequent references to his marriage contract and the action based on this contract are therefore, except for the obvious contrivances of the plot, more annoying than effective. They remind us of the earlier Angelo who has claimed our imagination and who will not let us go. The same thing is true of Isabella. The memory of the original Isabella causes acute resentment of the Duke's proposal of marriage. Whether we approve of extreme asceticism or not, the passion for chastity which Isabella expressed with such uncompromising conviction in the opening scenes of the play makes it impossible to believe that the same woman would ever willingly marry anyone. 'Get her to a nunnery,' one student snarled. Mary Lascelles points out that it is the very idleness of criticism to ask how this play's new-married couples will settle down together,[7] and it is certainly true that Shakespeare frequently ends his comedies with matches which no marriage counsellor would sanction. And yet none of the parties to his other matches are creatures endowed with personalities so fundamentally hostile to a stock romantic future as Isabella and Angelo. It is their earlier, unforgettable selves who, haunting the memory of their audience, ask how they could settle down with Mariana and the Duke. In fact, their own ultimate silences in this connection are eloquent enough to raise the question. I realize there may be textual omissions in the final scene, but Angelo's last lines in the play as it stands plead for justice, for consequences, for death:

> I crave death more willingly than mercy;
> 'Tis my deserving, and I do entreat it.
>
> (v. i. 474–5)

Angelo never once, in the text we have, expresses the slightest desire 'to marry a good woman and be happy'. Isabella's last lines are about Angelo's desire for her. She says not a single word about the Duke's proposal.[8] Given Shakespeare's powerful initial presentation of these characters and their own stubborn refusal to accept officially the futures assigned to them, it seems fair

[7] Mary Lascelles, *Shakespeare's 'Measure for Measure'* (London, 1953), p. 137. I am indebted to studies of the play by Miss Lascelles and by A. P. Rossiter throughout this chapter.

[8] F. R. Leavis (*The Common Pursuit* (London, 1952), p. 172) argues that we should willingly 'let Angelo marry a good woman and be happy', and we might— if Angelo himself ever expressed a desire to do so. The effect of Lucio's dramatic punishment might likewise be altered if Lucio verbally decided to accept and make the best of his fate, like the character tricked into marrying the witty whore in *A Chaste Maid in Cheapside*. But the characters in *Measure for Measure* express no resignation, much less enthusiasm, concerning their dramatic destinies. In *Shakespeare's Problem Comedies* (New York, 1931), pp. 106–7, W. W. Lawrence notes that Isabella does not formally assent to the Duke's proposal in the closing lines of the play, but he does not think that 'there is any doubt that Isabella turns to him with a heavenly and yielding smile'. I myself would prefer to see her turn away from him with a frowning sneer, and I do not see why my preference is any more (or less) subject to doubt than Lawrence's, since the text itself gives not one shred of evidence concerning Isabella's response.

enough for an audience to wish that Shakespeare had allowed them to face the truths and the consequences of dilemmas and desires which once seemed their own dramatic business—not the Duke's.

The real trouble with *Measure for Measure* begins when, in the course of some acutely human events, Shakespeare suddenly endows the Duke of Vienna with the superhuman, omniscient, manipulative powers of a Prospero—powers far beyond those of Marston's manipulator-spokesman, Malevole. An audience will readily accept superhuman intervention from benevolent manipulators like Oberon or Prospero, who initially demonstrate their power and announce that all will be well for the human mortals who enter their domains. But the same audience may justifiably question such intervention when a previously undistinguished character in a realistic dramatic context suddenly begins, half-way through the action, to exercise prerogatives that are traditionally associated with a dramatic divinity. There is just not enough evidence provided early in the play that Shakespeare's Duke (even to the degree of Marston's Duke Altofronto) can, wants to, or will be able to control the situation in festering urban (and suburban) Vienna. Indeed, the first motive the Duke gives for leaving the city is that the legal and social situation there has got out of his control and he wants somebody else to clean up the mess which his own permissiveness has created (I. iii. 19–43). This motive hardly entitles him (morally or dramatically) to put an objecting Angelo (I. i. 48–51) to a test, or to cause unnecessary suffering for a number of his subjects merely in order to find out what might lie behind Angelo's stony exterior (I. iii. 50–4). And if the Duke knew all along that Angelo had jilted Mariana, as he says later on (III. i. 206–17), he would hardly have needed to test Angelo for flaws in the façade. F. R. Leavis argues that we should not analyse the Duke as if he were 'a mere character, an actor among the others', but there is no evidence early in the play that he is anything more. In the long run we cannot analyse him as such because he will not stand up under the kind of analysis which we can give with no effort at all to, say, Lucio or Barnardine. So one alternative is to interpret the Duke allegorically, to see in him the workings of a mysterious Providence. But are a few allusions to Power Divine, a disguise as a priest, a speech informing us that the Duke has ever sought to know himself (III. ii. 218–19), really enough to exalt him, late in the action, to the status of a 'more-than-Prospero' as Leavis calls him?[9] I think not. He is much less than the real Prospero, who makes his powers and the limits of his powers clear, who analyses himself and controls himself along with the situation and the other characters. But I wonder, in fact, if any form of *deus ex machina* introduced in the third act of *Measure for Measure* could be successful, any more than some super-Polonius, disguised, providentially, as a priest, could, half-way through the play, convincingly manipulate Hamlet and Claudius into reconciliation and shift the action from revenge tragedy to comedic mercy. The personal conflicts and the intellectual dilemmas presented in the first acts of *Measure for Measure* are, like those in *Hamlet*, too deeply rooted for any happy resolution.

Indeed, the fundamental clash between the claims of the rule of law, the claims of abstract justice, and the claims of mercy which Shakespeare introduced in the opening scenes of *Measure for Measure* may not admit of any final solution at all apart from the tragic non-solution which the same conflicts produce in Melville's *Billy Budd* and which similar conflicts produce in the *Antigone*. In an imperfect world (and Vienna is notably imperfect) the realm of law is necessarily a realm of judgement and choice which dialectically conflicts with the realm of Christian idealism where all judgements are regarded ultimately as simple: Forgive your enemies; judge not that ye be not judged.[10] And Isabella's contrast between a god's or even an individual's renunciation of vengeance and a governor's enforcement of the law is an unfair one. Shakespeare knew this perfectly well. Henry V makes clear

---

[9] *The Common Pursuit*, p. 169. For interpretations of the Duke as Power Divine, and the play as a kind of Christian allegory, see G. Wilson Knight, '*Measure for Measure* and the Gospels', *The Wheel of Fire* (London, 1930), pp. 80–106, and the essays by Roy Battenhouse and R. W. Chambers (p. 58, n. 6, above).

[10] For a full account of the essential conflicts between the rule of law and theological mercy see Reinhold Niebuhr, *Love and Justice* (New York, 1967).

distinctions between divine mercy, an individual's renunciation of vengeance, and legal punishment:

> God quit you in his mercy! Hear your sentence.

> Touching our person seek we no revenge;
> But we our kingdom's safety must so tender,
> Whose ruin you have sought, that to her laws
> We do deliver you.
>   (*Henry V*, II. ii. 166–77)

Much of our annoyance with Duke Vincentio stems from his consistent refusal (and this refusal seems to be the most consistent thing about the Duke) to face up to the dilemmas and responsibilities of a governor who, whether he likes it or not, is bound to enforce the law. In other plays where the justice–mercy conflict arises, Shakespeare emphatically distinguishes between a ruler's personal pity and forgiveness and his duty to the law, even when the law is cruel or silly. 'We may pity, though not pardon thee' (*Comedy of Errors*, I. i. 98) is the typical statement of the Shakespearian governor. In *A Midsummer Night's Dream* Shakespeare explicitly contrasts the magical domain of Oberon, who is free from human law and necessity, with the realm of Theseus, who rules by the statutes of Athens:

> For you, fair Hermia, look you arm yourself
> To fit your fancies to your father's will,
> Or else the law of Athens yields you up—
> Which by no means we may extenuate—
> To death, or to a vow of single life.
>   (I. i. 117–21)

In *The Merchant of Venice* the Duke is very sorry for Antonio, and does his best to qualify Shylock's rigorous course, but Antonio himself realizes that 'The Duke cannot deny the course of law', and Portia agrees:

> . . . there is no power in Venice
> Can alter a decree established;
> 'Twill be recorded for a precedent,
> And many an error, by the same example,
> Will rush into the state.
>   (IV. i. 213–17)

And Escalus, the closest thing to a *raisonneur* in *Measure for Measure*, reminds us of the characteristic dilemma of a virtuous Shakespearian govenor:

> *Escalus.* It grieves me for the death of Claudio;
> But there's no remedy.
> *Justice.* Lord Angelo is severe.
> *Escalus.* It is but needful:
> Mercy is not itself that oft looks so;
> Pardon is still the nurse of second woe.
> But yet, poor Claudio! There is no remedy.
>   (II. i. 266–71)

This essential and dramatic clash between the law, justice, and mercy appears in *Measure for Measure* well before Angelo becomes obsessed with Isabella. Vienna is in a state of misrule because of the Duke's refusal to enforce the laws:

> We have strict statutes and most biting laws,
> The needful bits and curbs to headstrong steeds,
> Which for these fourteen years we have let slip;
> Even like an o'ergrown lion in a cave,
> That goes not out to prey. Now, as fond fathers,
> Having bound up the threat'ning twigs of birch,
> Only to stick it in their children's sight
> For terror, not to use, in time the rod
> Becomes more mock'd than fear'd; so our decrees,
> Dead to infliction, to themselves are dead;
> And liberty plucks justice by the nose;
> The baby beats the nurse, and quite athwart
> Goes all decorum.
>   (I. iii. 19–31)

So the Duke brings in Angelo, who rigidly enforces the letter of the laws on the books and arrests Claudio under an exceptionally severe old statute against fornication. Still, under the law, Claudio is guilty as charged, and though his pre-contract and intent to marry Julietta make the death penalty completely unjust, it is nevertheless perfectly legal. In her arguments with Angelo, Isabella never denies the legality of Claudio's sentence or even questions the validity of such a cruel statute ('O just but severe law!' II. ii. 41)—she appeals to Christian mercy. And Claudio himself blames 'too much liberty' for his current predicament. Given the situation in Vienna, Angelo's decision to enforce the letter of the law seems no less (though no more) acceptable than the Duke's repeated decisions to ignore law and pardon everybody on his criminal docket. In one case, severity plucks justice by the nose, in the other case, liberty does.[11] And, unlike the Duke, Angelo intellectually confronts the issues inherent in a judge's responsibility, and he makes some valid points in his arguments with Isabella:

> It is the law, not I condemn your brother.
> Were he my kinsman, brother, or my son,
> It should be thus with him.
>
> (II. ii. 80–2)

A cluster of Shakespearian associate justices—the Duke in *Othello* (I. iii. 67–70), Henry V and the Lord Chief Justice of England (*2 Henry IV*, v. ii. 70–117)—would assent to the impartiality of Angelo's enforcement of the law. And Angelo's statement about precedent,

> Those many had not dar'd to do that evil
> If the first that did th'edict infringe
> Had answer'd for his deed
>
> (II. ii. 91–3)

---

11 See Elizabeth M. Pope, 'The Renaissance Background of *Measure for Measure*', *Shakespeare Survey*, ii (1949), 74, who quotes a contemporary distinction between two kinds of equally bad judges. The first are men such as the Duke, 'such men, as by a certain foolish kind of pity are so carried away, that would have nothing but *mercy, mercy*, and would . . . have the extremity of the law executed on no man. This is the high way to abolish laws, and consequently to pull down authority, and so in the end to open a door to all confusion, disorder, and to all licentiousness of life.' The second kind are men such as Angelo: 'such men as have nothing in their mouths, but the *law*, the *law*; and *Justice*, *Justice*; in the meantime forgetting that Justice always shakes hands with her sister mercy, and that all laws allow a mitigation. . . . These men, therefore, strike so precisely on their points, and the very tricks and trifles of the law, as (so the law be kept, and that in the very extremity of it) they care not, though equity were trodden under foot.' There is a middle ground—equity—but its spokesman in *Measure for Measure* is Escalus, not the Duke (see Ernest Schanzer, *The Problem Plays of Shakespeare* (London, 1965), p. 116).

has strong support from the Duke's own original account of the legal and social mess in Vienna.

An exceptionally good gloss on the cruel legal dilemma surrounding Claudio appears in Melville's *Billy Budd*. Captain Vere is faced by the paradox that though the vicious Claggart was rightly struck down by Billy, 'the angel of God', the Mutiny Act requires that 'the angel must hang'. At the Last Assizes, Vere says, ultimate justice will acquit Billy. 'But how here?' he asks. In a navy threatened by spreading mutiny, Vere decides that he must proceed under the law of the Mutiny Act:

> For suppose condemnation to follow these present proceedings. Would it be so much we ourselves that would condemn as it would be martial law operating through us? For that law and the rigor of it, we are not responsible. . . . But the exceptional in the matter moves the hearts within you. Even so too is mine moved. But let not warm hearts betray heads that should be cool. Ashore in a criminal case will an upright judge allow himself off the bench to be waylaid by some tender kinswoman of the accused seeking to touch him with her tearful plea?[12]

Now the problems and the conflicts introduced in both *Measure for Measure* and *Billy Budd* are not essentially literary problems and conflicts. They are universally relevant social, human, and legal dilemmas which have, in this fallen world, no perfect social, human, or judicial solution. Laws can be cruel, they can go out to prey, they can bite, they can hurt. But without them liberty may become licence, the baby may beat the nurse, and headstrong steeds (or weeds) may run wild. Indeed Shakespeare's initial appeal to the facts of human experience represents a threat to certain theological ideals, for it reveals that the law set down in heaven, 'judge not that ye be not judged', offers no solution to the earthly problem. It is a spiritual law set down for mortals to obey when

---

[12] Ultimately, in this story, 'the condemned man suffered less than he who mainly had effected the condemnation'. Such is the potentially tragic dilemma of judges. For a contrasting view of what might be expected from an upright judge see W. W. Lawrence (*Shakespeare's Problem Comedies*, p. 114): 'an audience would hardly see virtue in a man who insisted on sending a youth to death for a venial offence, in the face of moving appeals for mercy uttered by a beautiful heroine.'

they renounce personal vindictiveness or choose tolerance. It has never been set down on earth as an explicit guide for the conduct of magistrates, for it would then be a commandment to command them from their function—it is their business to judge. Furthermore, in the first half of *Measure for Measure*, Shakespeare gives the Duke's permissiveness and Angelo's severity (for which the Duke's earlier permissiveness and retreat is responsible) equal blame for the grievous personal and social suffering displayed. Thus, when the Duke gives pardon to everybody in the end, there are all sorts of ghostly stage whispers chorusing 'Remember me' from the cellarage. They come from the reverberating echoes of earlier statements by the Duke, Angelo, and Escalus concerning precedent and the rule of law. And any argument that the Duke has somehow developed an intellectual and moral conviction that his earlier permissiveness was socially and legally justified all along is just as shaky[13] as an argument that the personalities and passions of an Angelo or an Isabella can be as readily and satisfactorily altered as stock comic humours—neither argument is supported by the text on the desk. Furthermore, if this Duke is Providence, his own continuing improvidence turns him, in the play as it stands, into a contradiction in terms.

For, both socially and dramatically, the Duke's decision to grant mercy to everybody revokes the rule of law, and to revoke the rule of human law is to revoke the idea of consequence, of necessity (the law may be a kind of dramatic metaphor for blind necessity in this play). It does not impose order (providential or otherwise) on the action, it imposes the disorder of incredibility. Of course it attempts to transform what is a fundamentally human and tragic situation into some sort of comedy, but whether this transformation is successful is a debatable point. Whether it is desirable is another one. As it is made in *Measure for Measure* the transformation deprives the characters (including the Duke) of human and dramatic dignity by denying them the full measure of responsibility that comes from facing the consequences of their own decisions and desires. And it deprives the audience of watch-

[13] See Clifford Leech, 'The "Meaning" of *Measure for Measure*', *Shakespeare Survey*, iii (1950), 69.

ing them make the terrible choices between equal claims to their
devotion. In effecting his final shift from a tragic to a comic mode,
Shakespeare, by breaching it, calls to our attention an essential
decorum described in a tale by Isak Dinesen:

[Tragedy is] a noble phenomenon, the noblest on earth. But of the
earth only, and never divine. Tragedy is the privilege of man, his
highest privilege. The God of the Christian Church Himself, when He
wished to experience tragedy, had to assume human form. And even
at that . . . the tragedy was not wholly valid, as it would have become
had the hero of it been, in very truth, a man. The divinity of Christ
conveyed to it a divine note, the moment of comedy. The real tragic
part, by the nature of things, fell to the executors, not to the victim . . .
Tragedy should remain the right of human beings, subject, in their
conditions or in their own nature, to the dire law of necessity. To them
it is salvation and beatification. But the gods, whom we must believe
to be unacquainted with and incomprehensive of necessity, can have
no knowledge of the tragic. When they are brought face to face with
it they will, according to my experience, have the good taste and decorum to keep still, and not interfere. . . . [And] we, who stand in lieu
of the gods and have emancipated ourselves from the tyranny of
necessity, should leave to our vassals their monopoly of tragedy, and
for ourselves accept the comic with grace. Only a boorish and cruel
master—a parvenu, in fact—will make a jest of his servants' necessity,
or force the comic upon them.[14]

In *Measure for Measure*, those lords of the theatre, Shakespeare and
his Duke, make a jest of their servants' necessity by interfering with
the tragic, by forcing the comic upon the characters and the
audience; and thus, as we shall see later, they call the validity of
this particular kind of tragicomedy into question. Certainly when

[14] See Isak Dinesen, 'Sorrow-acre', in *Winter's Tales* (New York, 1961),
pp. 52–3. See also A. H. Maslow, *Toward a Psychology of Being* (Princeton, N.J.,
1962), p. 198, who clearly distinguishes between living in a realm of the imagination which is free from the laws of necessity, in the 'inner psychic world' of love,
poetry, art, and fantasy, and 'living in and adapting to the non-psychic reality
which runs by laws [the individual] never made and which are not essential to
his nature even though he has to live by them'. By contrast with 'the more
effortful, fatiguing, externally responsible world of "reality", of striving and
coping, of right and wrong, of truth and falsehood', the world of the imagination
may be called 'Heaven'.

mercy is granted to Angelo it denies his (and our) pressing requests for necessity, for consequences:

> Immediate sentence then, and sequent death,
> Is all the grace I beg.
>
> (v. i. 371–2)

And by so frustrating the desire for consequences, for tragedy,
which he himself earlier created, Shakespeare may very well
increase it, since, over the years, whether they are common or
uncommon, Christian or agnostic, readers have found the ending
of *Measure for Measure* not only aesthetically and intellectually
unsatisfying, but personally infuriating. In this instance, critics as
temperamentally different as Coleridge and Dr. Johnson use the
same word—'indignation'. For Coleridge, the ending 'baffles the
strong indignant claim of justice', and Dr. Johnson believed that
'every reader feels some indignation when he finds [Angelo]
spared'.[15]

Prospero, as we all know, granted universal mercy too. But
Prospero set everybody free to pursue their private destinies, for
good or ill. In legal jargon, Prospero dismissed the jury and let
the defendants go. Similarly, Marston's Duke Altofronto simply
kicks out Mendoza and allows the other characters to pair off as
they choose. But Duke Vincentio limits the freedom of his subjects to the incongruous futures that he chooses for them. Barnardine is placed in the custody of a friar (v. i. 483–4). The severe
Angelo and the rakish Lucio are alike ordered into shot-gun
weddings. And then the Duke proposes marriage (of all things)
to Isabella. All this sounds closer to the comic sentences of *Volpone*
than to the comic release of *The Tempest*. But watching the action
of *Volpone*, we watch the characters create their own dramatic
designs and destinies, and they are permitted their own morality
or immorality. In *Measure for Measure* the Duke forces his own
arbitrary morality and his own dramatic designs upon the action.
F. R. Leavis argues that the Duke's total attitude 'is the total
attitude of the play'.[16] But where does the Duke articulate a 'total

---

[15] Coleridge and Johnson are quoted by George L. Geckle in 'Coleridge on
Measure for Measure', *Shakespeare Quarterly*, xviii (1967), 71–2.
[16] *The Common Pursuit*, p. 163.

attitude'? We watch the Duke appear severely righteous with Julietta (II. iii), condemning her 'most offenceful act'—without irony or sympathy—as 'a sin'. Then later we hear him tell Mariana that, since Angelo is her husband on pre-contract, "'tis no sin' for her to do virtually the same thing that Julietta did (IV. i. 70–1); and because no clear legal or moral distinctions between *de praesenti* and *de futuro* betrothals are given us, what appears to be simply a double standard on the part of the Duke is naturally confusing to any common sense of either justice or morality. Elsewhere we watch the Duke deliberately put Angelo to a test (I. iii. 50–4), then condemn him for failing it, and finally take the credit for forgiving Angelo while conveniently forgetting that he himself was directly responsible for Angelo's original predicament and therefore for all the suffering in the play. Prospero's situation was very different. Prospero's 'rarer action' represented his personal forgiveness of people who injured him personally. Prospero himself has suffered, and we watch him struggle to forgive. But so far as the text of *Measure for Measure* is concerned, the worst thing that the Duke of Vienna faces in his entire dramatic life is a series of rather amusing insults from Lucio. And the Duke finds these personal insults harder to forgive than any other offences in the play—major or minor, attempted or committed. But in his final judicial role, the person to compare the Duke with is not Prospero but Henry V, and the Duke does not come off very well. Henry readily takes into account extenuating circumstances and grants pardon to a drunk who slandered him personally; then he personally forgives the traitors, but he finally turns them over to the law. It is in *Henry V* and not in *Measure for Measure* that we find an upright judge who does his best to achieve a viable legal and human solution to the legal and human dilemmas inherent in his role as governor.

In order to justify the Duke as Providence Divine, or the Image of an Ideal Ruler, or a Compliment to James, it becomes necessary to transform Shakespeare from the greatest of poets into the kind of philosopher that Sidney set beneath the poet: 'I say the *Philosopher* teacheth but he teacheth obscurely so as the learned onely can understand him, that is to say, he teacheth them that are alreadie taught.' The poet, in contrast, 'beginneth not with obscure definitions which must blurre the margent with interpretations, and loade the memorie with doubtfulnesse'. Now on a literal (as opposed to any symbolic) level, Shakespeare's Duke has much less in common with either Providence Divine or an Ideal Ruler than he has in common with Ben Jonson's tyrant Tiberius. Jonson's enigmatic Emperor and Shakespeare's Duke of dark corners both deliberately retire from view and in doing so they get 'seconds' (Angelo and Sejanus) to do their political dirty work for them. Later on they both write contradictory letters, and finally they manifest their full power and overthrow their deputies. But Jonson's tyrant obviously represents neither Providence Divine nor an Ideal Ruler. In the words of *Sejanus*, a tyrant 'is a fortune' sent to test the virtue of Roman citizens. Gradually, in the course of the action, Jonson equates the inconsistent, arbitrary behaviour of Tiberius with the inconsistent, arbitrary behaviour of the Roman deity Fortune. In parallel scenes, Fortune and Tiberius turn away from Sejanus, and we learn in the end that Tiberius, not Sejanus, has turned fortune's wheel in Rome from the very beginning. But Tiberius does not himself change his mode of behaviour. We are simply given progressively fuller information about him that changes our attitudes towards him and incorporates his modes of behaviour into the over-all meaning of the play. Shakespeare's Duke changes his attitudes and actions as the plot requires, moving from incompetence to omniscience, from advocating severity to advocating leniency, with no modulation in between.

No matter how hard we try to incorporate the Duke's behaviour into some over-all interpretation of the play, all the incorporation and all the interpreting appears to be ours—not Shakespeare's. If, uncertain how to justify the intrusion of his *deus ex machina* and unable to resolve the essential dilemmas of the first acts without doing so, Shakespeare made his text hard to follow because of *non sequiturs*, contradictory moral attitudes, impressive-sounding references to Power Divine, and elaborate in-jokes to compliment James, then we shall have great difficulty in finding out exactly what Shakespeare intends us to understand. We shall have to reason it out much as we reason out a notice in some language we do not fully understand. Thus some pretty strenuous reasoning may be interposed between the author's conceptions and our interpretation of them, and it is strangely easy to forget that in this specific instance the reasoning was not Shakespeare's, but all our own.[17] The strenuous reasoning behind most of the critical justifications of the Duke, behind all the allegorical and historical interpretations of *Measure for Measure*, appears to me to have been done by individual critics rather than by Shakespeare, who, in the text as it stands, seems to treat the Duke with something like poetic contempt. For while he lavishes great poetry on the early Angelo, Isabella, and Claudio, and while he treats them, even in their moments of extreme cruelty or cowardice, with great dramatic sympathy, he never gives the Duke a speech which is not self-contradictory or contradicted by the action itself. In fact, the reader in search of the tritest lines in the play, or even the tritest lines in the complete works of Shakespeare, need look no further than the Duke's summing-up of *Measure for Measure*. The same final lines issue a command just as silly and as unenforceable as the legal commandment against fornication. The Duke says 'Love her, Angelo'. Now if human biology cannot be subjected to magisterial command, neither can human emotion. Love your enemies and forgive them if you can. But do not command them to love you, or to love each other. Not even Prospero, Shakespeare's most powerful dramatic manipulator, commanded or expected that. King Lear learned the folly of such commandments too. But Duke Vincentio learns nothing. He admits no limits to his power and he never once analyses the total situation. And so, in defiance of all our critical efforts, Duke Vincentio, in the second half of *Measure for Measure*, remains outside any meaning, an external plot-manipulator, a dramatic engineer of a comic ending, who never sees beyond his single theatrical goal.

[17] I have applied to *Measure for Measure* the same treatment that P. B. Medawar gives to obscure modern philosophical writing in 'Science and Literature', *Encounter* (January 1969), p. 19. Medawar concludes that 'in all territories of thought which science or philosophy can lay claim to, including those upon which literature has also a proper claim, no one who has something original or important to say will willingly run the risk of its being misunderstood'.

Thus, precisely because of the Duke, throughout the final scene of *Measure for Measure* I feel great sympathy for Angelo, who was placed in a position to be tempted, given a dramatic appetite, then cheated of the satisfaction of gratifying it and piously condemned because he tried to do so. The play is comparable to a lady who first deliberately excites desire, then refuses to satisfy it. The ending implies that we ourselves should overcome any temptation to demand consequences and retributive justice, just after it has provocatively tantalized us with precisely this temptation. If Shakespeare wished to lead us, in the course of this play, from an appetite for tragedy (for *Hamlet*) to an appetite for comedy (for *The Tempest*) this is not the way to do it, and this specific experiment in tragicomedy is a magnificent failure. The rarer action may be in virtue than in vengeance, but we like to choose virtue for ourselves; we do not like having virtue thrust upon us any more than we like to see it thrust upon characters who are not born virtuous and do not achieve virtue for themselves in the course of the action. Indeed we may rebel against virtue imposed more than against punishments imposed. For if the facts of life have always rebelled against conventional poetic justice because it simply is not true that virtue is inevitably rewarded and vice always punished, it is even less true that divine or ducal intervention will finally make everybody be good. And do we, in fact, truly want everybody to be good at the dramatic price exacted from us by the Duke?

One school of modern criticism, on its knees before the Duke, overlooks the obvious fact that the Duke's protection ultimately forces personal and dramatic diminution on those he protects. It forces the awesome Angelo to lie down in the second-best bed of the faceless Mariana, and it blithely passes this off as the best of all dramatic destinies. At the very same time that it shelters the characters from the ultimate consequences of their own decisions and desires, it denies them the dramatic magnificence which comes only from facing such consequences. And it deprives the audience itself of an ultimate dramatic confrontation with the terrible facts of life, with the crushing dilemmas, the human vice, the human pathology which all lurk in the wings at the end of *Measure for*

Measure but which the Duke, by ignoring them, tries to keep out of our sight. Indeed the Duke would seem to have precisely the same essentially patronizing designs upon us that he has upon Isabella: his palpable didactic design attempts to make us feel merciful, and his mechanical comic design attempts to make us forget the reality and the suffering of the first half of the play. For these reasons, it is good and proper that Isabella and Angelo remain silent at the end. In the 1970 production of the play at Stratford, Isabella, with stunning effect, remained alone on the stage at the end. It would be equally interesting to see Angelo coolly manifest resentment and contempt as he stands before the Duke, for this would dramatically deprive the Duke of his all too easy victory, leave Angelo with his original individuality, and lend the impact of truth to the conclusion:

> Forgive me not, Vincentio,
> My will remains my own;
> You know it not, but I well know
> I still remain Lord Angelo,
> By choice myself alone.[18]

Still, in the long run, the violence of all these aesthetic, intellectual, and emotional objections to *Measure for Measure* testify to the play's continuing power. It is impossible to forget either its power to hurt or the things it most did show. But here any analogy with Sonnet 94 breaks down, since even some of the bravest dramatic weeds cannot outbrave the dignity of Shakespeare's festered lily. Who would prefer to have written *The Malcontent* if he could have written the great first half of *Measure for Measure*? Nevertheless, the fact remains that *The Malcontent* works as a whole, while *Measure for Measure*, taken as a whole, leaves us all knotted up in a snarl of contradictions. The play appears to show us that extremism in the pursuit of anything (chastity, sex, mercy, law) causes such damage that it becomes a vice. But at precisely the same time, the play emphatically demonstrates that while extremism in the pursuit of chastity, sex, or law may produce very

---

[18] My apologies to Mr. Auden.

great drama, extremism in the pursuit of a happy ending most definitely will not. Similarly, in defiance of the Duke's decisions (which suggest that they will suffice) the over-all action of the play demonstrates that the laws set down in heaven will not work down here on earth. And likewise, in defiance of its artificial reconciliations, the play haunts us with the cruel fact that there may be totally irreconcilable contradictions between equally valid claims to human devotion. *Measure for Measure* also clearly reveals that there are certain equally irreconcilable contradictions between comic and tragic form. For this particular tragicomedy amounts, in structure, to a dramatic self-contradiction.

In *The Malcontent* Marston took a satiric *via media* between comic and tragic form, and the result is a consistent dramatic intrigue which is governed by a consistent satirical perspective. Likewise, the dramatic realm of *The Tempest*—ruled by magic and governed with benign, philosophical detachment—transmutes comic and tragic elements alike into a rich and strange substance of its own. But the first half of *Measure for Measure*, so far as its major characters are concerned, is exclusively tragic, while the second half is a network of comic intrigues. And these two dramatic modes of presentation admit no more reconciliation than the original conflict between Isabella's desire to maintain her own chastity and her desire to save her brother's life. A decision between them is necessary; and where its major characters decide for tragedy, the play decides for comedy. But if comedy gets the last word, tragedy gets the first word, and the first word prevails because it is more powerfully expressed poetically and dramatically, and also because the word rings true. The first half of the play shows us what is in fact the case; the second half is escapist fiction. Indeed it may be a fact of dramatic life that without magic, and certainly without a clear, consistent, imaginative modulation or assimilation of them, the literal facts of human necessity, human evil, and human passion will inevitably threaten any moral or dramatic idealism that guarantees that All will be Well, and assumes that all things are but easy when they are known. For if, as Leavis argues, in the second half of the play the Duke affords us a 'criticism of life', the facts of life in the first half of the play afford us with a devastating criticism of the ducal contrivances of the second half. For Vincentio's realm was vividly introduced as a threatening world of striving and failing, of choices and judgements, a world of necessity, where people are condemned by laws they never made—in short, as the world we know. The second half of the play is thus doomed to fail the test of truth when it attempts to replace, reject, or ignore the nature of its own original dramatic dispensation. And so, and still, the phoney dramatic solution imposed upon this play's problems only calls our attention to its own ineffectuality, and thus unofficially makes us notice what we are apparently not officially supposed to notice. For by so abruptly moving into the conventionally theatrical realm of *The Malcontent*—the realm of intrigues and the expulsion of humours—only after powerfully exhibiting a series of insoluble human dilemmas, the play creates its own insoluble artistic dilemmas. And this is its major problem. And this is where we came in.

One kind of aesthetic experience creates the appetite for a different kind, and after a confrontation with *Measure for Measure*— a play which involves us personally, emotionally, intellectually, and morally, and poses problems on all these levels—it is a refreshing change to turn to a Restoration comedy which holds us morally at arm's length and sets out, without any apologies, to entertain us with some enduringly fashionable and fascinating human vices and follies. There are times when a play like Etherege's *The Man of Mode* can satisfy a very genuine dramatic need, otherwise

> In Briton why shou'd it be heard,
> That Etheredge to Shakespeare is preferr'd?
> Whilst Dorimant to crowded audience wenches,
> Our Angelo repents to empty benches: . . .
> The perjur'd Dorimant the beaux admire;
> Gay perjur'd Dorimant the belles desire:
> With fellow-feeling, and well conscious gust,
> Each sex applauds inexorable lust.[19]

[19] Steele, 'Epilogue to *Measure for Measure*', quoted by Joseph Wood Krutch in *Comedy and Conscience After the Restoration* (New York, 1924), p. 245.

Steele's Epilogue to *Measure for Measure* goes on to cry 'For shame!' and to ask his readers to 'scorn the base captivity of sin'. I shall make no such request of mine. In fact the whole gist of my discussion of *The Man of Mode* may be introduced by echoing some conventional wisdom: when faced by attractive and amusing immorality (in art, of course) it is best to relax and enjoy it.

4 'Vice under characters of advantage': dramatic and social success in *The Man of Mode*

I perceive the Laws of Religion and those of the *Stage* differ ex-
treamely.   JEREMY COLLIER

Lying, Child, is indeed the Art of Love; and Men are generally
Masters in it.   CONGREVE

THE reader who turns from *Sir Fopling Flutter, or The Man of
Mode* to certain recent discussions of this comedy is due for
a sobering experience. For instance, any frivolous mirth occa-
sioned by the play would tend to be dampened by Jocelyn
Powell's argument that the play shows the emptiness of Dorimant's 'life of isolation', and 'All the devices of comedy, charm,
cleverness and wit, encourage one to laugh with Dorimant at his
victims, but the sympathy with which those victims are themselves
described make us aware that the approval we have been giving
through our laughter is of what we hate. We are given a double
view of the situation, a view of the pretence, and of the truth,
and before it we are helpless, aware that our intellectual and
emotional responses form a devastating contradiction.' For James
Sutherland, 'Without Sir Fopling . . . *The Man of Mode* would be
almost a dark comedy', since 'It is Dorimant, a Restoration Don
Juan and almost too intense a personality to be the hero of a
comedy, who dominates the play . . . He never wastes a word, his
comments are devastating, and he has a detachment and self-
control that put all the other characters, except Harriet, at his
mercy. Even Harriet's courage and self-possession occasionally
tremble on the verge of defeat, and the duel between the two
generates an unusual tension.' For Dale Underwood, the activities
of Dorimant are 'explicitly' and 'predominantly' the expression

of 'a Hobbesian aggressiveness, competitiveness, and drive for power and "glory"; a Machiavellian dissembling and cunning; a satanic pride, vanity, and malice; and, drawing upon each of these frames of meaning, an egoistic assertion of self through the control of others'.[1] It seems to me that the righteous solemnity of these passages distorts Etherege's comic emphasis on the Ovidian game and art of love—an emphasis which deserves more discussion later. Also, these descriptions of Dorimant sound more suited to a Volpone, an Iago, or even Satan, than to Etherege's 'genteel rake of wit',[2] and the fact that they do so raises some elementary critical questions. Can the recognition of traits that are shared by a whole range of comic and, for that matter, tragic characters—Tamburlaine, Richard III, Volpone, Macbeth, Iago, Satan, Dorimant, Maskwell, the Vicomte de Valmont, Julien Sorel, Sammy Glick, and James Bond, to name just a few—give us very much insight into any single one of these characters? Or do these traits represent *données* of characterization, points of departure from which writers move on to develop their characters into tragic, heroic, comic, sympathetic or villainous individuals?[3]

[1] See Jocelyn Powell, 'George Etherege and the Form of a Comedy', *Restoration Theatre, Stratford-upon-Avon Studies 6*, ed. J. R. Brown and Bernard Harris (London, 1965), pp. 61, 68; James Sutherland, *English Literature of the Late Seventeenth Century* (Oxford, 1969), pp. 110–11; Dale Underwood, *Etherege and the Seventeenth-Century Comedy of Manners* (New Haven, Conn., 1957), p. 73. The same severity appears in Norman Holland's description of the country, which, he says, 'as a place highly unpleasant because close observation forces the inner self to conform to visible mores' is therefore a 'suitable House of Holiness for Dorimant's penance' (*The First Modern Comedies* (Cambridge, Mass., 1959), p. 93). Charges of triviality and irrelevance to the best thought of its time, which have been directed at Restoration comedy in general by L. C. Knights, in 'Restoration Comedy: The Reality and the Myth', *Explorations* (London, 1946), pp. 131–49, may have influenced modern criticism to discuss and defend Etherege's comedy with undue solemnity. For the sake of argument, I have deliberately selected quotations that illustrate the moralistic tone of modern discussions of this play; but everyone who has read the studies in which they appear knows how valuable they are.

[2] Dr. Lockier's description of Dorimant in Joseph Spence, *Observations, Anecdotes and Characters, of Books and Men*, ed. Edmund Malone (London, 1820), p. 115.

[3] See Charles Lamb's plea that Richard III be not reduced to his vices ('On the Tragedies of Shakespeare' in *The Works of Charles and Mary Lamb*, ed. Thomas Hutchinson (Oxford, 1908), p. 135): 'A horror at his crimes blends with the

Furthermore, the very vices Underwood names may, on the stage or in the study and even, occasionally, in life, appear embodied in figures so attractive that moral judgement is merged with aesthetic enjoyment, intellectual appreciation, and even emotional admiration of them.

Indeed, audiences have often delighted in characters whose behaviour and attitudes shock them, in characters who have the pride, energy, intelligence, cunning, or power to overleap moral fences and to invert traditional values. And certainly playwrights have always enjoyed creating such characters, perhaps taking it for granted that what would outrage the moral philosopher might nevertheless please an audience—that, like themselves, their audiences would just as soon imagine an Iago as an Imogen, a Dorimant as an Emilia. It is mainly in judicious retrospect that characters whose vices do become them represent a combined critical and moral dilemma to their audience; for a different order of theatrical salvation and damnation can take place on the stage down here, where, in the course of the action, Falstaff, Richard III, and Cleopatra always steal the show (and the audience) from the Lord Chief Justice, Richmond, and Octavia—characters who have all the moral virtues but none of the theatrical ones.[4]

Nevertheless, in retrospect, it may be disturbing that the most appealing characters in a given play not only outrage accepted moral standards but (what is worse) seem to enjoy themselves

effect which we feel, but how is it qualified, how is it carried off, by the rich intellect which he displays, his resources, his wit, his buoyant spirits, his vast knowledge and insight into characters, the poetry of his part,—not an atom of all which is made perceivable in Mr. C.'s way of acting it. Nothing but his crimes, his actions, is visible; they are prominent and staring; the murderer stands out, but where is the lofty genius, the man of vast capacity,—the profound, the witty, accomplished Richard? . . . While we are reading any of [Shakespeare's] great criminal characters . . . we think not so much of the crimes which they commit, as of the ambition, the aspiring spirit, the intellectual activity, which prompts them to overleap those moral fences.'

[4] Also, 'There's a great deal of difference betwixt likeing the Picture and the Substance. A Man may be very well pleas'd with a Forest work piece of Tapestry, with the Lyons, the Bears, and the Wolves, &c. but not over fond of their Company in Flesh and Blood; and consequently the very worst Jilt may be the Minion upon the Stage, and, as I said before, our Aversion off it' (Elkanah Settle, *A Defence of Dramatick Poetry* (London, 1698), p. 88).

thoroughly in the process of doing so, whether or not they are punished in the end.[5] A sensitive spectator who might have held mixed emotions in solution during the course of the play is likely, when it is over, to feel some need to choose between these emotions, to decide—critically and morally—whether his attitude towards dramatic vice should be disapproval or admiration; to choose between being glad or sorry a character got what was coming to him in the end, or between being glad or sorry the character got off scot-free in spite of his misdeeds. Frequently it is hard for critics to make up their minds which of these attitudes is the proper one, or even to decide which attitude the playwright intends us to adopt. Does a playwright, in glamorizing vice, thereby condone or commend it? Or does he, by exposing the vice behind the glamour, thus condemn it?

Answers to these questions necessarily differ from play to play, from critic to critic, and from time to time, and the questions themselves are very old and very obvious ones. But they are questions which almost inevitably arise to influence discussions of Restoration comic playwrights who so frequently and so blatantly present pleasure in alliance with vice, and 'vice under Characters of Advantage',[6] that the immorality, morality, or amorality of their plays has been a continuing subject of controversy. Attacking Restoration playwrights for their encouragement of vice, Jeremy Collier accuses them of lavishing all their wit and art on their libertine characters; and, in doing so, he gives us a pretty accurate description of a character like Dorimant: 'A finish'd Libertine seldom fails of making his Fortune upon the *Stage* . . . there is great Care taken to furnish him with Breeding and Address: He is presently put into a Post of Honour, and an

[5] Punishment at the end need not negate the impression created by the dramatic presentation of fashionable vice during the course of the action. The anonymous author of *The Stage Condemn'd* (London, 1698), p. 80, gives an amusing account of the theatrical allure of vice: 'such is the Nature of Vice . . . that if either the Pleasure, or Ease, or Prosperity and Success of it be shewn and acted, though but for a few Minutes, whatever Fate it ends in . . . it leaves a pleasing Impression behind it, nor is the After-Clap, or doleful Exit of it, strong enough to prevent a liking or satisfaction.'

[6] Jeremy Collier, *Dissuasive from the Play-House* (London, 1703), p. 4.

Equipage of Sense; and if he does the worst, he is pretty sure of speaking the best Things; I mean the most lively and entertaining.'[7] Dorimant also fits the pattern described by Sir Richard Blackmore, who, like Collier, is outraged by the way playwrights may present 'a Person wholly *Idle*, dissolv'd in Luxury, abandon'd to his Pleasures, a great Debaucher of Women, profuse and extravagant in his Expences' as a '*Fine* Gentleman', as 'the chiefest Person propos'd to the Esteem and Imitation of the Audience', who is 'enrich'd with all the Sense and Wit the Poet can bestow'.[8] Collier and Blackmore clearly recognize and deplore the libertine vices that modern critics find characteristic of Dorimant, but their subsequent emphasis differs sharply. Where modern critics stress Etherege's dramatic exposure of libertine vice, the seventeenth-century writers take the vices for granted and go on to stress, while they bewail, the fact that playwrights do everything in their power to make the possessors of these vices attractive enough to lead astray the audience itself. And somehow the argument that playwrights who create glamorous libertines really are moralists out to expose the vices of their characters seems less true to the spirit of *The Man of Mode* than an argument that Etherege, dramatically at least, condones the conspicuously immoral behaviour of his main character. Certainly he systematically and constantly associates Dorimant's libertine activities and attitudes with 'grace, dignity, spirit, a high social position, popularity, literature, wit, taste, knowledge of the world [and] brilliant success' with the ladies. The words just quoted are Macaulay's, who argues that uniting vice and attractiveness is a very bad thing for a playwright to do,[9] but who, like Collier, seems to give a demonstrably truthful account of what Etherege does do with his libertine hero in *The Man of Mode*.

Within Etherege's comic context, Dorimant is the 'Loveliest of those Libertine Pictures', the 'amiable Counterfeit' of a 'Fine Gentleman' (like Rochester) who, when the play begins, is

[7] Ibid.

[8] Preface to *Prince Arthur*, in J. E. Spingarn (ed.), *Critical Essays of the Seventeenth Century* (Oxford, 1909), vol. iii, p. 230.

[9] See *Critical and Historical Essays by Lord Macaulay*, ed. F. C. Montague (London, 1903), p. 12.

London's undefeated champion in the game of love. The excite-
ment of the comedy, and much of the fun, comes from watching
the skill with which he and his partners play the game—from
watching him handle his 'Cooling Intriegue' with Loveit, his
'Amour, *en passant*', with Bellinda, and then from seeing him
finally meet his match in Harriet.[10] Like the activities in which
Dorimant engages, the play in which he appears is obviously
trivial compared to the most profound thinking and writing of its
time (compared, say, to *Paradise Lost*), just as Ovid's *The Art of Love*
is trivial compared to *The Aeneid*. In fact, the two comparatively
trivial, frivolous, and immoral works have a good deal more in
common with each other than they have in common with the
deeply serious writings of their eras. They both adopt the same
attitude towards their major subject—love affairs—and Dorimant's
attitudes and patterns of behaviour are all recommended en-
thusiastically in *The Art of Love*, where "tis [but] a Venial Sin to
cheat the Fair; / All Men have Liberty of Conscience there'.[11] If
Dorimant enjoys seductions, dissembling, and making ladies
passionately furious ('I have not had the pleasure of making
a Woman so much as break her Fan, to be sullen, or forswear her
self these three days'—I. i. 203–5),[12] so does Ovid:

> We sin with Gust, we love by Fraud to gain;
> And find a Pleasure in our Fellow's Pain.
>
> (p. 36)

Throughout the play, Dorimant treats Loveit in exactly the way
Ovid recommends:

> Oft make her jealous, give your Fondness o'er,
> And teaze her often with some new Amour.

---

[10] Quotations are from Settle's discussion of *The Man of Mode* in his *Defence of Dramatick Poetry* (n. 4 above), p. 92—hereafter cited as Settle.

[11] From Ovid's *The Art of Love*, trans. Dryden, Congreve, and others (London, 1747), p. 32. Page numbers citing this translation, which is the most generally accessible of the several Restoration translations, hereafter will be inserted in the text. John Wain points out Ovidian assumptions in Congreve in his 'Ovid in English' (*Preliminary Essays* (London, 1957), p. 76), though he does not mention Ovid in his interesting discussion of *The Man of Mode* in the same volume.

[12] Quotations from *The Man of Mode* are from *The Dramatic Works of Sir George Etherege*, ed. H. F. B. Brett-Smith, vol. ii (Oxford, 1927).

Happy, thrice happy Youth, with Pleasures blest,
Too great, too exquisite to be exprest!
That view'st the Anguish of her jealous Breast.
Whene'er thy Guilt the slighted Beauty knows,
She swoons; her Voice, and then her Colour goes.
Oft would my furious Nymph, in burning Rage,
Assault my Locks, and with her Nails engage;
Then how she'd weep, what piercing Glances cast!
And vow to hate the perjur'd Wretch at last.

(p. 92)

Like Ovid's nymph, Loveit vows hatred and rages, but she always
comes back for more: 'I had rather be made infamous by him,
than owe my reputation to the dull discretion of those Fops you
talk of' (II. ii. 49–51). Dorimant also follows an Ovidian formula,

Tho' *Ætna's* Fires within your Bosom glow,
Dissemble, and appear more cold than Snow,

(p. 203)

when he conceals his growing love from Harriet—'I love her, and
dare not let her know it' (IV. i. 151)—and of course Harriet follows
suit by concealing her feelings from him: 'I feel as great a change
within; but he shall never know it' (III. iii. 66–7). With Bellinda,
where his own feelings are always under control, Dorimant
follows a different Ovidian stratagem; he 'acts well the lover', and
lets his 'Speech abound / In dying Words' (p. 30): 'Nothing is
cruel to a man who could kill himself to please you' (III. ii. 72–3),
'By all the Joyes I have had, and those you keep in store . . . Ever-
lasting love go along with thee' (IV. ii. 22–3, 67–8). And if Dorimant likes to have at least two mistresses at a time (even after he
has promised to join Harriet in the country he flirts with Bellinda
and Loveit), this, too, follows an Ovidian maxim:

If to Excess you find your Passion rise,
I would, at once, two Mistresses advise . . .
Who can at once two Passions entertain,
May free himself at Will from either Chain.

(p. 201)

Immoral though it may be to feign indifference when you feel
passion, and to appear ardent when you really are casual, these

essentially Ovidian rules of conduct govern Dorimant's behaviour in Etherege's light comedy, which, like *The Art of Love*, treats love as a kind of warfare, and as a game. On the level of amorous warfare, Etherege, like Ovid, gives us examples of logistics, tactics, scouting expeditions, skirmishes, campaigns, victories, defeats, and peace treaties. Like a game, love has its rules, and (again like Ovid) Dorimant and his fellow players provide examples of winners, losers, points scored, bluffs, penalties, and ties. Characters in *The Man of Mode* are awarded their prizes and penalties according to their mastery of those rules of old discovered (not devised) by Ovid, and subsequently proclaimed effective by a succession of authorities on the game of love from the Comte de Versac and Madame de Merteuil to (Stendhal's) Prince Korasoff and Mae West. The penalty incurred by Loveit provides a good example.

Where Dorimant and Harriet know the rules and principles of love, and artfully put them into practice, Loveit knows the theory, but artlessly lets her passions prevail over her sense and strategy. She knows perfectly well that jealousy may revive a waning love ('Love, when extinct, Suspicions may revive'—Ovid, p. 149), that the only way to renew Dorimant's interest is to make him jealous: '[Jealousy is] the strongest Cordial we can give to dying Love, it often brings it back when there's no sign of life remaining' (III. iii. 211–13). And until she departs from this formula and admits to Dorimant that she despises Sir Fopling, the Ovidian prescription works perfectly. Dorimant does get jealous, and his interest does revive:

> *Dor.* She cannot fall from loving me to that!
> *Med.* You begin to be jealous in earnest.
> *Dor.* Of one I do not love—
> *Med.* You did love her.
> *Dor.* The fit has long been over—
> *Med.* But I have known men fall into dangerous relapses when they have found a Woman inclining to another.
> *Dor.* He guesses the secret of my Heart! I am concern'd, but dare not show it, lest *Bellinda* should mistrust all I have done to gain her.
> (III. iii. 296–306)

Dorimant successfully conceals his concern from Bellinda; but Loveit, a few scenes later, allows Dorimant to pluck off her mask and to see the 'passion that lies panting under' and thus she forfeits the game: '*Dissimulation* is part of the essence of *Complaisance*, without which 'tis impossible that a Courtier or any other person should be able to conduct himself with safety amidst the malice and contrivances of men, for he who knows not how to conceal his game, gives great advantage to those he plays with . . . [like] those gamesters who shewing their Cards occasion their own loss.'[13] Dorimant is rewarded for his successful dissembling (he gets Bellinda), and Loveit is penalized for her 'want of needful Art' (Ovid, p. 128)—she loses Dorimant. To allow passion to overrule one's sense is, in the game of love, to become the horse instead of the charioteer, the bull instead of the matador. Her lack of control is the cause of Loveit's woes: 'It is thus, that those who abandon themselves to Love without consulting Reason, find themselves constrained to confess their blindness and errour with shame to all the World.'[14] One may feel sorry for Loveit, but this is something like feeling sorry for a defeated player in a chess match; the pity comes from criteria other than the standard of the game which he did not play successfully enough to win, and thus deserved to lose. Technical and tactical errors always involve penalties within a comic context where skill in the game of love has everything to do with success, and where goodness has no- thing to do with it. Dorimant himself has to accept his penalty when he miscalculates and is caught by Bellinda at Loveit's lodgings: 'There is no remedy, I must submit to their Tongues now, and some other time bring my self off as well as I can', 'You have reproach't me handsomly, and I deserve it for coming hither' (v. i. 275–7, 289–90). Old Bellair should not even try to play. He makes a glorious fool of himself through his bumbling attempts to feign dislike for Emilia, which only serve to reveal his excessive admiration for her charms: 'He calls me Rogue,

[13] From 'S. C.', *The Art of Complaisance* (London, 1673), pp. 8–9.
[14] See *The Art of Making Love: or, Rules for the Conduct of Ladies and Gallants in their Amours* (London, 1676), p. 55. The peculiar mixture of Ovid and Casti- glione which appears in this book provides an amusing commentary on Restora- tion comedy and tragedy.

tells me he can't abide me, and does so bepat me', says Emilia, and this convinces Lady Townley that 'he has a doating Fit upon him' (II. i. 10–11). Still, in Harriet's words, 'because some who want temper have been undone by gaming, must others who have it wholly deny themselves the pleasure of Play?' (III. iii. 49–51).

In contrast to Loveit and Old Bellair, Harriet always plays with enjoyment and finesse. She delights in the 'dear pleasure of dissembling' (III. i. 120), never reveals her hand, and is so equally matched with Dorimant that the result of their encounters is always a tie. She artfully puts barriers in Dorimant's way, feigns indifference, mixes 'sweetness' with 'severity', and is so 'malitiously ingenious' that by little favours she nourishes Dorimant's desire without 'easing or satisfying it'[15] beyond 'a little harmless discourse in publick walks, or at most an appointment in a Box barefac'd at the Play-House' (III. iii. 70–2)—nothing more without 'church security'. With skill and relish, she follows the rules for a fine lady engaging in a love affair: 'let a Lady act with so much prudence, that she may gain the perfect knowledge of her Lover's heart before she trust . . . and, to appear more amiable, she seems inhumane, and ofttimes counterfeits an excessive Pride, the better to charm with her Caresses.' Thus, 'in despising Love at the first', Harriet triumphs 'with the greater power',[16] matching Dorimant's wit, sang-froid, and glamour with her own.

Like Dorimant, Harriet shows no pity for her defeated opponent. She is even more scornful of Loveit than Dorimant, and she, too, could be described, in Mr. Underwood's vocabulary, as aggressive, proud, competitive, and cunning. In fact, allowing for variations in tactics, all three ladies—Loveit, Bellinda, and Harriet—play to win. If Dorimant (like Ovid) warns against trusting male friends, women are not to be trusted either. Bellinda, who contrives the initial trick on her friend, is as treacherous to Loveit as Dorimant: 'Thus justly Women suffer by Deceit; / Their Practice authorises us to cheat' (Ovid, p. 32). Loveit and Bellinda, in fact, explicitly demand even more exclusive sovereignty over Dorimant than Harriet, who, when he offers to give up his interest in all other women, shrewdly says she wants him devout,

---

[15] *The Art of Making Love*, p. 48.   [16] Ibid., pp. 129–31.

but not fanatic. However, all three ladies are alike in their goal:
'The veriest Wanton of that Sex is as much for *Monopoly* as the
other; they care not for half Hearts, a Gallant divided between
a *Lovet*, a *Bellinda*, and a *Harriot*.'[17] If Dorimant is out to conquer
them, they are out to conquer him. This is one reason why we
need not worry too much when Dorimant tries to do to them
what they would like to do to him (or to each other), and
why an amused, impersonal fascination with the way they play
their game seems a more enjoyable attitude towards these characters than a distressed concern for their moral and ethical short-
comings.

Immorally, but, I think, deliberately, Etherege's comic organization is designed to excite admiration for the ability to dissemble
successfully. All his best people do it. Young Bellair, a thoroughly
nice boy, is most amusing and attractive when he is gulling his
father with Harriet. Harriet has feigned obedience to her mother
in order to get to London (III. i. 40), she and Young Bellair fool
their parents with skill and with great pleasure, and she matches
Dorimant's cool nonchalance with her own. Dorimant and
Bellinda dupe Loveit, and Dorimant goes on to dissemble to
practically everybody else. Enjoying himself enormously in the
process, Dorimant plays the taunting master with Loveit, the
irresistible rake with Bellinda, the conservative gentleman, Cour-
tage, with Lady Woodvil, and the honourable suitor with Harriet.
This comedy puts a premium on acting ability, and punishes most
severely the major character least capable of acting—Loveit.
Perhaps it might be argued that a treatment of Ovidian love,
which demands continual acting, is ideally suited to comic drama.
Certainly the art of love and the art of the theatre can merge
significantly in a play where the characters are so conscious of
behaving artificially. The very qualities which Ovid recommends
for success in love, the very qualities which Dorimant possesses—
the sang-froid and the talent for dissembling which make it
possible for him to evoke emotion in others while remaining
detached himself—are the qualities that have been considered
essential for success on the stage. For instance, according to Diderot,

[17] Settle, p. 84.

'Ce n'est pas l'homme violent qui est hors de lui-même qui dispose de nous; c'est un avantage réservé à l'homme qui se possède.
. . . Ce n'est pas son cœur, c'est sa tête qui fait tout . . . tout son talent consiste non pas à sentir, comme vous le supposez, mais à rendre si scrupuleusement les signes extérieurs du sentiment, que vous vous y trompiez.'[18] The better to counterfeit the ideal image of the character he plays, the actor must coolly calculate his every gesture, every speech: 'Celui donc qui connaît le mieux et qui rend le plus parfaitement ces signes extérieurs d'après le modèle idéal le mieux conçu est le plus grand comedién.'[19] In this connection, Betterton, making every word and gesture manifest the ideal Dorimant, the ideal fine gentleman, acted out on the stage essentially the same ideal that was acted out, successfully, in life, by Rochester and aspired to by Etherege himself.

In *The Art of Love*, the *Paradoxe sur le comédien*, and *The Man of Mode* the traditionally immoral 'art' of dissembling is a highly desirable one, which is rewarded with social success, and the peculiar way such a specifically theatrical value and skill becomes transformed into a social and personal value and skill seems to be an important feature of literature and life in Restoration England and eighteenth-century France: 'Celui qui dans la société se propose, et a le malheureux talent de plaire à tous, n'est rien, n'a rien qui lui appartienne, qui le distingue, qui engoue les uns et qui fatigue les autres. Il parle toujours, et toujours bien; c'est un adulateur de profession, c'est un grand courtisan, c'est un grand comédien' (Diderot, p. 297). In this connection it is illuminating to compare Diderot's instructions to actors throughout the *Paradoxe sur le comédien* with discussions about acting in real life which appear in Ovid, Laclos's *Liaisons dangereuses*, and *The Man of Mode*. Ovid advises:

> In spite of Torture, still from Tears refrain;
> Laugh when you have most reason to complain . . .

---

[18] From Diderot's *Paradoxe sur le comédien*, in *Diderot's Writings on the Theatre*, ed. F. C. Green (Cambridge, 1936), pp. 256-8.

[19] Ibid., p. 297. My discussion of Diderot is indebted to a series of conversations with Peter Brier, who pointed out that Diderot's theory and Restoration comic practice have a good deal in common.

But Counterfeit; You'll prove in the event,
That careless Lover whom you represent.

(p. 203)

Similarly, Madame de Merteuil concludes:

In vain I had been told and had read that [love] could not be feigned;
I saw that to do so successfully one had only to join the talent of
a comedian to the mind of an author. I practised myself in both arts
and perhaps with some success; but instead of seeking the vain applause
of the theatre, I resolved to employ for my happiness what others
sacrifice to vanity. . . . Did I experience some grief, I studied to show
an air of serenity, even one of joy; I carried my zeal so far as to cause
myself voluntary pain and to seek for an expression of pleasure at the
same time. I worked over myself with the same care and more trouble
to repress the symptoms of an unexpected joy.[20]

And Harriet asks Dorimant: 'Did you not tell me there was no
credit to be given to faces?—That Women nowadays have their
passions as much at will as they have their Complexions, and put
on joy and sadness, scorn and kindness, with the same ease they
do their Paint and Patches?'

If, throughout *The Man of Mode*, Dorimant is always very
conscious of the way he will 'act', so, apparently, were his creator
and various members of his audience in the theatre as well as his
fellow characters on the stage. Like the actors who play them,
Dorimant and the other characters in Etherege's play receive
rewards or punishments according to their successful realization
of their roles, according to the success of their efforts to evoke the
responses they wish to evoke, and not according to the morality
or immorality of their parts: 'In fine, 'tis the Wit of the Composure, not the Vice in the Composure, gives life to the Comedy.
A dull Representation of Vice or Virtue, shall be equally Hist off
the Stage.'[21] Theatrically, the role of Sir Fopling is a fine one

[20] *Les Liaisons dangereuses*, Letter lxxxi, tr. Richard Aldington (London, 1925),
pp. 223–6.

[21] Settle, p. 87. He adds that ' 'Tis not the Lewdness it self in a Vicious Character,
that recommends it to the Audience, but the witty Turnes, Adventures and
Surprizes in those Characters that give it Reception. For without this, the Play
drops and dies.'

because it provides the actor and the audience with such a superb image of a Fop, and not because Sir Fopling is good-natured; while ultimately it is the dramatic fascination inherent in libertine and Ovidian assumptions, and not the moral faults inherent in these assumptions, which gives their embodiment, Dorimant, the centre of the stage.

Better, I think, to relish Dorimant's dissembling, his Ovidian intrigues, his expertise, and his occasional discomfiture, than to turn the comedy into a sermon against the character it so clearly wants us to enjoy, or to impose traditional moral considerations upon a play that sets out so gaily to flaunt them. I wonder if any amount of critical argument can finally gainsay the impression given in the course of the action that Dorimant—with all his vices made so conspicuous that they can be taken for granted—is a comic hero who evokes appreciation rather than the genial ridicule that is directed at Old Bellair and Sir Fopling, Etherege's comic targets. Nevertheless, Dale Underwood argues that Old Bellair and Sir Fopling themselves provide us with norms of honour and good nature by which the vices of Dorimant should be measured. Old Bellair wants to marry Emilia, and Mr. Underwood thinks this is 'pointedly honorable' in contrast to Dorimant's interest in an affair with her. But is it? Like other old men who have wanted to marry pretty young girls in comedies, Old Bellair, however good-natured he may be, is something of a dirty old man, and very much a fool to wish to marry the girl who marries his son. Better an affair with Dorimant than marriage to Old Bellair, from most points of view within the play; and in fact the latter would almost inevitably lead, in the course of time, to the former. Sir Fopling, says Mr. Underwood, is repeatedly 'rejected by the wiser fools as they acclaim the hero, whose surface good humor conceals his natural malice'.[22] But the other characters do not so much reject Sir Fopling as enjoy his unsuccessful efforts to play the Fine Gentleman. And is it not possible that their favourable opinions of Dorimant are there simply to establish the general nature of his popularity and appeal? The character who most disapproves of Dorimant is Lady

[22] *Etherege and the Seventeenth-Century Comedy of Manners*, pp. 81, 85.

Woodvil, herself a comic target, who later succumbs to his charm.

Granted that we need a modern approach to Restoration comedy, is it really necessary to require an Etherege *moralisé* in order to enjoy *The Man of Mode*? The games people play in Etherege's comedy are timeless (if trivial) ones, and like *The Art of Love*, *The Man of Mode* is still amusing and relevant enough on its own terms. It seems unnecessary to deplore the amorous intrigues of rakes and flirts in such a light comedy unless the comedy itself specifically calls for a harshly moral attitude towards its characters—an attitude which the Ovidian norms and the dramatic emphasis of *The Man of Mode* seem designed to preclude. In a different play moral evaluations of the characters may be quite appropriate. In *The Way of the World* the values of *The Man of Mode* are held up to question and found wanting. But the best way to enjoy Etherege's comedy seems to be to follow the advice given in its prologue, and 'be not too severe'. Recognizing all Dorimant's rakish ways, John Dennis, in his *Defense of Sir Fopling Flutter* declares that 'all the World was charm'd with *Dorimont*', and describes *The Man of Mode*, very accurately, I think, as 'one of the most entertaining Comedies of the last Age, written by a most ingenious Gentleman, who perfectly understood the World, the Court, and the Town'.[23]

Dennis's praise seems to me to be much truer to the spirit of *The Man of Mode* than the moralistic interpretations of modern critics. For the light comic spirit pervading the play allows us

[23] See *The Critical Works of John Dennis*, ed. Edward Niles Hooker, vol. ii (Baltimore, 1943), pp. 248, 242. Dennis is refuting Steele (*Spectator*, 65), whose arguments that Dorimant is 'a direct Knave in his Designs', and that 'nothing but being lost to a Sense of Innocence and Virtue can make any one see this Comedy, without observing more frequent Occasion to move Sorrow and Indignation, than Mirth and Laughter', are similar to those of the modern critics cited earlier. Dennis answers that while Dorimant is very obviously 'a young Courtier, haughty, vain, and prone to anger, amorous, false, and inconstant', he is, after all, the hero in a comedy, and comedy never has been much concerned with paragons of virtue. Within Etherege's entertaining context, Dennis says, Dorimant provides 'an admirable Picture of a Courtier in the Court of King Charles the Second . . . *Dorimont* not only pass'd for a fine Gentleman with the Court of *King Charles the Second*, but he has pass'd for such with all the World, for Fifty Years together' (pp. 244–5).

to look at the social spectacles that it mirrors and magnifies and see them as—spectacles. The primary purpose of this comedy seems to be neither immoral nor moral, but rather spectacular— to exhibit, rather than to censure, the features of fashionable vice, fashionable virtue, and unfashionable folly, and to show their interaction in a glittering, amusing, and witty dramatic spectacle. And if the play reveals that fashionable vice and fashionable virtue frequently were one and the same when the play was written, just as they are now, this is true to the subject and important to the spectacle. For the more elegantly, spectacularly, rakish the rake (the more foppish the fop, the more dejected the rejected mistress) the better. Since Mrs. Barry (who made the part of Loveit so much her own) could play passionate women with great fire, the more passionate her part, the better. Betterton's own elegance and sex appeal projected across the footlights and so (like its counterpart on the stage) all the world was charmed with Dorimant. Traditional morality has nothing to do with all this. And traditional morality remains outside the imaginative focus of Etherege's comedy precisely because traditional morality is not spectacularly portrayed within it.

Traditional morality is not portrayed spectacularly in *Antony and Cleopatra* either, and a primary concern with the spectacular, as opposed to a primary concern with morality, is not unique to Restoration comedy. Shakespeare, says Coleridge, 'had read nature too heedfully not to know that courage, intellect, and strength of character were the most impressive forms of power, and that to power in itself, without reference to any moral end, an inevitable admiration and complacency appertains, whether it be displayed in the conquests of a Napoleon or Tamerlane, or in the foam and thunder of a cataract'.[24] The drama's inevitable concern with the spectacular, in all its forms and for its own sake, may be the main reason why moralists have attacked the drama throughout its history, and why so many failed efforts to moralize drama clutter up the same history. For the drama mirrors the spectacular in life itself, and the spectacular is not necessarily the moral—not down

[24] *Coleridge's Shakespearean Criticism*, ed. T. M. Raysor, vol. i (London, 1930), p. 58.

here in the theatre of the world. It therefore is futile to argue that dramatists do not load their dramatic dice in favour of their most spectacular characters. They may do so obviously or subtly, consciously or unconsciously, but they do it all the time. Etherege's dramatic dice are loaded in favour of Dorimant and there is no point in arguing that Young Bellair *really* represents Etherege's dramatic ideal, since, within the comedy itself, the rake gets all the lines. 'Who gets all the lines?' is not a silly question to ask about a play. The answer may be very obvious but because it is very obvious it is likely that it may also be very revealing. For the success or failure of a play is dependent upon the immediate responses which it commands within the theatre itself, and the over-all emphasis of a play, even a very subtle play, must make itself evident before the final curtain. Thus to argue that some subordinate, easily overlooked, easily forgotten characters can significantly refute, qualify, or obliterate a play's primary emphasis is to turn minor co-ordinates into major ones. For while it is true that Young Bellair is a very nice boy, his minor role gives him no real opportunity to challenge our primary response to Dorimant.

Certainly when, where, and if—but only when, where, and if—morality is important to the dramatic purposes of a playwright, the playwrights themselves make morality itself spectacular. A glance at some Shakespearian dissemblers comparable (as such) to Dorimant can illustrate this fact. Shakespeare himself makes Macbeth's moral awareness and suffering just as spectacular and moving as possible. A moral recognition shadows every immoral action of this man, who never for one moment enjoys collecting his wages of sin. On the other hand, Richard III loves collecting his. He is determined to prove a villain and by proving himself such a spectacular villain he releases us from any moral need to prove him one. Where Macbeth's moral nature rebels in horror against his own mutation into a hell-hound, against his own tragic fate, Richard's immoral nature exults in his dramatic destiny:

> March on, join bravely, let us to it pell-mell;
> If not to heaven, then hand in hand to hell.
>
> (v. iii. 312–13)

Richard gleefully enjoys his own spectacular vices, and so do we. But nobody else on the stage enjoys them. For Richard is placed within a larger frame of reference, a context of nemesis, of history, of guilt and suffering, a context which lends grim irony to his (and our) enjoyment of his spectacular actions. In contrast to Richard, Iago is the arch-enemy of the spectacular. He is diabolically jealous of it. Thus he is frequently the spokesman for ordinariness, for statistical reductions and promotions by grade, and thus he sets out to destroy the spectacular whenever he finds it—to destroy heroic love, heroic virtue, heroic poetry. This is one good reason why he is so much more chilling and despicable than either Richard or Macbeth, who both commit far more murders. They are on the side of the spectacular. Within their dramatic worlds, they are the embodiments of it. Iago, in the world of *Othello*, is its nemesis.

Dorimant's domain is dramatically worlds apart from the realms of any of these dissemblers, but within his own sphere he is the embodiment of the spectacular. Dorimant's sphere itself differs significantly from the spheres of Shakespeare's dissemblers. It differs according to Etherege's subject, which is not the tragic destruction (and tragic renewal) of a great love, nor the anguish of a damned soul, nor the cruelly necessary instruments of history and retribution, but social and amorous intrigues. And this diversity of subject gives diversity of signification to Etherege's specific dissembler, to the play's master of social and amorous intrigues. Dorimant experiences no moral retribution of any kind. He does get his comic come-uppance, but the limits of his power are defined by Harriet, the play's mistress of social and amorous intrigues, his ultimate partner and adversary in the game of love. The irresistible force meets the immovable object (and vice versa) and the game will go on in the country. If we wish it to, a comedy like *The Man of Mode* may instruct us—but not about moral crime and punishment. It may instruct us about its historical social scene, and about the comparable social scene we all know, about the masks people wear, and about the way people play the game of love. And its creator does explicitly instruct us. He instructs us to sit back and relish both the spectacle on the stage and the spectacle round about. For he is a comic poet, and (in the words of Dennis) 'a true Comick Poet is a Philosopher, who, like old *Democritus*, always instructs us laughing'.[25]

William Congreve also fits Dennis's definition, and Congreve's masterpiece, *The Way of the World*, is by all odds the most instructive of Restoration comedies. Now, while it seems astonishing that modern criticism should need to be reminded that Congreve is primarily a comic poet, precisely this reminder seems necessary in the face of a critical movement to read his works (and other Restoration comedies as well) as if they were solemn theological treatises. These days it is highly fashionable to find profound moral and theological significance in the religious imagery which appears all over the place in Restoration comedy. Recent interpretations of Congreve's *Love for Love* and—yes indeed—*The Man of Mode* have stressed the crucial significance of their religious allusions. Before this critical movement goes any further, it seems time to pause for a minute and ask just exactly how far interpretations of these comedies which are based on their religious imagery really will take us towards their specific comic truths, or rather, bluntly to ask whether the current critical effort to read plays, as Congreve's Jeremy says 'they read hard *Hebrew* books backwards', does not in fact 'begin to read at the wrong end'.

[25] Dennis, p. 250.

5 'Diversity of signification': religious imagery in restoration comedy and secular reality in *Love for Love*

> When a man looketh upon the rules that are made he will think there can be no faults in the World; and when he looketh upon the faults there are so many he will be tempted to think there are no rules.
>
> A man that steps aside from the World, and hath leisure to observe it without interest or design, thinks all mankind as mad as they think him for not agreeing with them in their mistakes.   HALIFAX

HERE is a recent critical generalization about Congreve's plays: 'The plays of William Congreve . . . are all, in their various ways, the beautifully carved images of a Providential justice that governs all human affairs, even those that occur in the most sophisticated and flirtatious drawing-rooms.'[1]

And here is one possible response to this generalization. If Congreve's plays are beautifully carved images of a providential justice that governs all human affairs, they are then monuments to a dead idealism, so why read them? Surely all the evidence of sense and experience denies that there is any justice (providential or otherwise) governing 'all human affairs'. There may be appropriate rewards and punishments in a comedy. There may be appropriate rewards and punishments for us all in some after-life. But a glance around makes it glaringly apparent that no over-riding justice governs affairs in the world we know. Therefore, do we really want to accept a dramatic image of a providential

---

[1] See Aubrey Williams, 'Poetical Justice, the Contrivances of Providence, and the Works of William Congreve', *Journal of English Literary History*, xxxv (1968), pp. 540–1. But see also Robert Ornstein, *The Moral Vision of Jacobean Drama* (Madison, Wis., 1960), p. 13: 'Just as the apologist for the stage can find a moral in the most prurient play, so too the pious can interpret the resolution of any dramatic fable as a demonstration of Providence.'

justice which does not exist in the place of Congreve's brilliant comic representation of the way of the world that does exist? For within the drawing-rooms of Congreve's greatest comedy, it takes a lot more than Providence to outwit Mr. Fainall and Mrs. Marwood. It explicitly and literally takes experience, foresight, a knowledge of character, and actions specifically calculated to restrict the enemy's power to hurt. And this literal level of truth concerning the way of the world is what this particular comedy (and the next chapter) is all about.

Nevertheless, in Congreve's earlier *Love for Love*, Valentine clearly informs Tattle that 'you would have interposed between me and Heav'n; but Providence laid Purgatory in your way— You have but Justice' (v. i. 595–7).[2] Furthermore, along with this reference to Providence, *Love for Love* is crowded with allusions to traditional religious conceptions. There is Miss Prue's 'catechism'; Valentine's repeated insistence, 'I am Truth'; numerous references to 'martyrdom' of various types; and names with scriptural connotations—Sampson, Ben, Angelica. So may we not reach conclusions about *Love for Love*, at least, which are based on detailed consideration of its religious imagery? The answer is no. For it is easy to demonstrate that the evidence for any such conclusions—the religious imagery itself—may be interpreted in too many different ways, all depending upon the assumptions of the individual critic who is interpreting it. For instance, the same reference to providential justice and the same religious imagery which are considered so profound in modern discussions of *Love for Love* were considered offensively profane by seventeenth-century moralists. In fact, Congreve's virtual elimination of any religious imagery from *The Way of the World* (1700) was almost certainly the result of Jeremy Collier's tirade of 1698 against the profanity of the scriptural allusions which he found in Congreve's earlier plays, and particularly in *Love for Love* (1695).

Given the furore aroused by Collier's *Short View of the Immorality and Profaneness of the English Stage*, it is not surprising

---

[2] Quotations are from *The Complete Plays of William Congreve*, ed. Herbert Davis (Chicago, 1967).

H

that Congreve, who surely intended to amuse, not to offend, was
disturbed by Collier's attack on his religious allusions in *Love for
Love*[3] and therefore deliberately left religious imagery out of
The Way of the World. Attacking Restoration comedy for its
immorality, Collier had cried out that the 'Language of the *Scriptures*' and the 'most solemn Instances of Religion' were 'prosti-
tuted to Courtship and Romance'[4] in *Love for Love* and other
comedies. According to Collier, any hint of burlesque directed
at scriptural meaning caused people to laugh when they should
tremble at the blasphemy, and he finds the exalted vocabulary of
the Scriptures degraded when it is associated with the explicitly
secular and frequently bawdy subject-matter of Restoration
comedy. *Love for Love*, says Collier, will give us an 'account of this
Authors Proficiency in the *Scriptures*. Our Blessed Saviour affirms
himself *to be the Way, the Truth, and the Light, that he came to bear
witness to the Truth, and that his Word is Truth*. These expressions
were remembered to good purpose. For *Valentine* in his pretended
Madness tells *Buckram* the Lawyer; *I am Truth,—I am Truth.—
Who's that, that's out of his way, I am Truth and can set him right.*
Now a *Poet* that had not been smitten with the pleasure of
Blasphemy, would never have furnish'd Frensy with Inspiration;
nor put our Saviours Words in the Mouth of a Madman.'[5]
Collier also deplores the verbal play on Sir Sampson Legend's
name. Quoting Angelica's warning to Sir Sampson, '*Have a care—
If you remember the strongest* Sampson *of your Name, pull'd an old*

---

[3] According to John C. Hodges, Jeremy Collier's attack on his plays stirred
Congreve 'more deeply than anything else in his career'. See Hodges's *William
Congreve, The Man* (New York, 1941), p. 62.
[4] Jeremy Collier, *A Short View of the Immorality and Profaneness of the English
Stage* (London, 1698), p. 76—hereafter cited as *Short View*.
[5] *Short View*, p. 83. Even a defender of Restoration drama was opposed to
explicit scriptural allusions in plays, and found 'smut' less offensive than blasphemy: 'No Story, no Phrase, no Expression whatsoever in the Bible, may be
repeated, or so much as alluded to, without Sin.... There is no trifling, no jesting,
with a Text of Scripture, but what will infallibly end in sad and woful earnest ...
yet there are some certain Vices, or rather seeming Vices, which *Mr. Collier*
however will not allow of, such as Smut, and those By-Words, which he calls
Oaths, which properly enough may, and very naturally do fall under the Cog-
nizance of the Comick Poet.' See Edward Filmer, *A Defence of Plays: or, The
Stage Vindicated* (London, 1707), pp. 64–5.

House over his Head at last', Collier argues that 'here you have the
Sacred History burlesqu'd, and *Sampson* once more brought into
the House of *Dagon*, to make sport for the *Philistines!*'[6] But above
all, Collier bewails the fact that the vocabulary of the Scriptures
is applied to amorous affairs in *Love for Love*: 'To draw towards
an end of this *Play*. *Tattle* would have carried off *Valentine's*
Mistress. This latter, expresses his Resentment in a most Divine
manner! Tattle, *I thank you, you would have interposed between me
and Heaven, but Providence has laid Purgatory in your way*. Thus
Heaven is debas'd into an Amour, and Providence brought in to
direct the Paultry Concerns of the *Stage!*'[7]

   Times have changed since Collier wrote, and so have interpretations of the religious allusions and vocabulary in Restoration
comedy. Modern critics (Norman Holland, Aubrey Williams,
Dale Underwood, and others) have concluded that religious
references lend ironic depth and moral dimension to *Love for Love*
and *The Man of Mode* since they point towards a traditional level
of values more sublime than the social, economic, and erotic
values which otherwise appear to govern the characters in these
comedies. Discussing the conclusion of *Love for Love*, Norman
Holland argues that when Angelica accepts Valentine after he has
resigned both his love and his money for her sake, Valentine 'sees
her then as a kind of religious fulfillment', an idea which is
'implicit, of course, in her name'. The religious imagery of the
play develops in the finale, says Holland, to reveal that 'the end
of Valentine's education is to bring him to a higher kind of
reality, a Providence or God's justice, that transcends the chance
and show of ordinary social reality'.[8] In support of this interpretation, Holland quotes the play's final lines:

Scandal. . . . there is a Third good Work, which I, in particular, must
thank you for; I was an Infidel to your Sex; and you have converted
me . . .
Angelica. . . . Men are generally Hypocrites and Infidels, they pretend to Worship, but have neither Zeal nor Faith: How few, like

---

[6] *Short View*, p. 76.   [7] Ibid.
[8] Norman Holland, *The First Modern Comedies* (Cambridge, Mass., 1959),
p. 164.

Valentine, would persevere even unto Martyrdom, and sacrifice their
Interest to their Constancy! . . .

> The Miracle to Day is, that we find
> A Lover true: Not that a Woman's Kind.

Ironically, Jeremy Collier sees exactly the same implications that
Holland sees in these lines, but Collier is outraged by Valentine's
'martyrdom': 'Here you have a Mistress made God Almighty,
Ador'd with Zeal and Faith, and Worship'd up to Martyrdom!'[9]
On the Restoration stage, Collier says,

> The Hero's Mistress is no less than his Deity. She disposes of his
> Reason, prescribes his Motions, and Commands his Interest. What
> Soveraign Respect, what Religious Address, what Idolizing Raptures
> are we pester'd with? *Shrines* and *Offerings*, and Adorations, are nothing
> upon such solemn Occasions. Thus Love and Devotion, Ceremony
> and Worship, are Confounded; And God, and his Creatures treated
> both alike! These Shreds of Distraction are often brought from the
> *Play-House* into Conversation: And thus the *Sparks* are taught to
> Court their Mistresses, in the same Language they say their *Prayers*.[10]

Where Holland finds an affirmation of religious values in Valentine's martyrdom, Collier finds an inversion of the same values.
Where Holland concludes that 'a Providence or God's justice' is
asserted, Collier finds it deplorable that 'Providence is brought in
to direct the Paultry concerns of the *Stage*'. Because these critics
are arguing from opposite premisses, they interpret the same
evidence in opposite ways.

Writing about *The Man of Mode*, Dale Underwood, rather like
Jeremy Collier, finds the association of Christian imagery with
the social and amorous concerns of Restoration comedy incongruous. But where Collier believes that the vocabulary of religion
is debased by the subject, Underwood argues that Christian
imagery serves to clarify the deficiencies of the other values projected in Restoration plays. According to Underwood, the ironic
contrast between Christian values and the values of Dorimant
makes clear the flawed nature of Dorimant's values. When
Harriet asks Dorimant, 'Could you keep a Lent for a Mistress?'
and Dorimant answers, 'In expectation of a happy Easter', Under-

[9] *Short View*, pp. 76–7.   [10] Ibid., pp. 282–3.

wood decides that their lines have significant ramifications for Etherege's plays. According to Underwood, the

> Lent–Easter witticism embodies, in fact, the whole ironic grace–fall–regeneration archetype which characterizes the total comic structure of the plays. And the comment it makes upon the world of the play summarizes the general import of both the Christian abstractions and the Christian imagery. It summarizes, indeed, the central import of Etheregean comedy. . . . At the surface of the image is, of course, a set . . . of distinctly Christian assumptions which also have courtly applications: repentance, atonement, and rebirth. At these levels alone, the point is obvious. The application of either courtly or Christian values to the world of Dorimant makes a sufficient comment in itself. . . . And Dorimant's 'Easter' is scarcely, at this stage at least, either courtly or Christian. The disparity underlines with greater firmness than in the earlier plays the unquestionable deficiencies of the comic world projected. And it catches the central ironies of character, action, and values in the play: the definition of the comic world by traditional frames of value which reveal not only its character but its inconsistencies and its deficiencies; the ambiguity of the curve of action (from grace to fall, or from fall to grace); the comic uncertainty of man as to either his own nature or his own desires.[11]

But if the application of Christian values to the world of Dorimant criticizes his world, why does not the application of Christian values to the world of Valentine and Angelica criticize theirs? Apparently, religious imagery, if nothing else, can be all things to all men. When critics want to, they can interpret it as ironic criticism; when they prefer, they can see it as a method of encompassing a literal love-affair within a higher reality; when they like, they can rail against its blasphemy. Alternatively, they can find it rather witty. Defending the drama against Collier's attack, Edward Filmer admits that the Lent–Easter passage from *The Man of Mode* is profane and smutty, but he concludes that smut and profanity, so urbanely expressed, are not offensive:

> *Mrs. Herriot*, a lively, brisk young Heiress; but withall a Person of great Honour, and Virtue, being Courted by *Dorimant*, a Gentleman of

---

[11] Dale Underwood, *Etherege and the Seventeenth-Century Comedy of Manners* (New Haven, Conn., 1957), pp. 105–6.

Sense, Wit, and Breeding, tho' otherwise a libertine: After some Discourse goes on thus.

> Herr. *To men who have fared in this Town like you, 'twou'd be a great Mortification to live on Hope: Cou'd you keep a Lent for a Mistress?*
> Dor. *In Expectation of a happy Easter, and tho' Time be very precious, think forty Days well lost, to gain your Favour.*

Now, tho' the first hint be here given by a Woman; and both Question, and Answer, are at the Bottom Smutty and Prophane, yet is there nothing in either, so plain or gross, as may seem to border, in the least, on Rusticity, or ill Manners.[12]

Defending his plays against Collier's attack, Congreve himself offers some help in interpreting the true nature of the religious imagery which so frequently appears in Restoration comedy: 'I desire that the following Distinction may be admitted, *viz.* That when Words are apply'd to sacred things, and with a purpose to treat of sacred things; they ought to be understood accordingly: But when they are otherwise apply'd, the Diversity of the Subject gives a Diversity of Signification.'[13] Though under extreme provocation, Congreve never suggests that his religious vocabulary elevates the subject to which it is applied. Quite the contrary. He says the vocabulary changes its import to conform with the subject to which it is applied. Nothing would have been more convenient for him, in his situation, than modern arguments that religious imagery lends ironic depth or moral profundity to his comedies. But these arguments apparently never entered his mind. When Scandal tells Mrs. Foresight, 'he will *die a Martyr rather than disclaim his Passion*', Congreve says that 'the word Martyr is here used Metaphorically to imply Perseverance. *Martyr* is a Greek word, and signifies in plain English, no more than a *Witness*. A holy Martyr, or a Martyr for Religion is one thing; a wicked Martyr, or Martyr for the Devil is another: A Man may be a Martyr that is a Witness to Folly, to Error, or Impiety. *Mr. Collier* is a Martyr to Scandal and Falshood quite through his Book.'[14] Congreve justifies his use of the same word

---

[12] Filmer, *Defence of Plays*, pp. 14–15.
[13] Congreve, *Amendments of Mr. Collier's False and Imperfect Citations* (London, 1698), p. 11.   [14] Ibid., p. 48.

in reference to Valentine's sacrifices for Angelica with exactly the same argument justifying the word in connection with Scandal's behaviour,[15] and his interpretation of Valentine's conduct is absolutely literal. According to Congreve, Valentine 'has Generosity and Sincerity enough, in the last *Act*, to sacrifice every thing to his Love; and when he is in danger of losing his Mistress, thinks every thing else of little worth. This, I hope, may be allow'd a Reason for the Lady to say, *He has Vertues*: They are such in respect to her; and her once saying so, in the last *Act*, is all the notice that is taken of his *Vertue* quite thro' the play.'[16]

What conclusions can we draw from these opposing interpretations of religious imagery apart from the depressingly consistent conclusion that a given religious allusion can mean whatever a critic wants it to mean? One conclusion is that, however interpretations of it may vary, before Collier's attack there was a good deal of such imagery in Restoration comedy. A casual glance over the epilogues to *Love for Love* and *The Old Batchelor* supplies us with plenty of it:

> Sure Providence at first, design'd this Place
> To be the Player's Refuge in distress;
> For still in every Storm, they all run hither,
> As to a Shed, that shields 'em from the Weather.
>
> .   .   .   .
>
> Methinks, we *Players* resemble such a Soul,
> That, does from Bodies, we from Houses strole.
> Thus *Aristotle's* Soul, of old that was,
> May now be damn'd to animate an Ass;
> Or in this very House, for ought we know,
> Is doing painful Penance in some *Beau*.
>
> .   .   .   .
>
> But we can't fear, since you're so good to save us,
> That you have only set us up, to leave us.
> Thus, from the past, we hope for future Grace . . .

Here we have Providence, salvation, damnation, and grace all brought in to advertise the new playhouse, but it would be

[15] Ibid., p. 55.   [16] Ibid., pp. 88–9.

far-fetched to conclude from Mrs. Bracegirdle's lines that Congreve
wanted to give us yet another beautifully carved image of 'a Providential justice that governs all human affairs'. Mrs. Bracegirdle's
lines are too arch, too flippant, for that. Nor will Mrs. Barry's
references to Lent, penitence, a fall, and damnation in her Epilogue
to *The Old Batchelor* lead us very far towards some cosmic level of
truth:

> As a rash Girl, who will all Hazards run,
> And be enjoy'd, tho' sure to be undone;
> Soon as her Curiosity is over,
> Would give the World she could her Toy recover:
> So fares it with our Poet; and I'm sent
> To tell you, he already does repent:
> Would you were all as forward, to keep Lent.
>
> .   .   .   .
>
> Yet, may be, you'll encourage a beginner;
> But how?—Just as the Devil does a Sinner.
> Women and Wits are used e'en much at one;
> You gain your End, and damn 'em when you've done.

Like Restoration comedy, seventeenth-century libertine poetry
is full of religious imagery. The idea of 'love's martyrdom' is
a commonplace in poetry and drama, and the same vocabulary
that Angelica uses for Valentine's zeal and martyrdom appears
in some explicitly obscene poems by Etherege:

> This may suffice to let you know
> That I to cunt am not a foe,
> Though you are pleased to think me so;
> 'Tis strange his zeal should be in suspicion
> Who dies a martyr for's religion.
>
> My zeal does my devotion quite destroy:
> Come to the temple where I should implore
> My saint, I worship at the sacred door.[17]

Does Etherege's religious vocabulary here reflect the 'whole
ironic grace–fall–regeneration archetype' which Mr. Underwood

---

[17] From 'Mr. Etherege's Answer' and 'Imperfect Enjoyment', in *The Poems of
Sir George Etherege*, ed. James Thorpe (Princeton, N.J., 1963), pp. 7, 43.

finds characteristic of his plays? Do the religious terms reveal 'the ambiguity of the curve of action (from grace to fall, or from fall to grace); the comic uncertainty of man as to either his own nature or his own desires'? Certainly not in a very portentous way, if at all. And how much more weight can we give to Angelica's lines concerning Valentine's zeal and martyrdom than we give to these lines, or to Scandal's statement to Mrs. Foresight that he would rather 'die a Martyr than disclaim his Religion'? If it is conspicuously true that Jeremy Collier made mountains out of molehills when he attacked the profanity of such lines, it seems equally true that modern critics make a different range of mountains out of the same molehills when they argue for their profundity.

In the end, Congreve's plea for interpretation in context provides the only sound solution to the problem of religious imagery in Restoration comedy. We know, since the play as a whole proves it, that Valentine's love for Angelica is truer than Scandal's love for Mrs. Foresight. The whole context of a play or a poem—profane or profound as it may be—should govern the interpretation of the individual lines that make it up. Since its religious vocabulary does not necessarily lend high seriousness to Etherege's poem about 'Imperfect Enjoyment', a similar vocabulary probably does not lend cosmic seriousness to *The Man of Mode* or *Love for Love* either. Interpretations of these comedies which argue that the invocation of some higher reality is primary to their meaning skate on pretty thin ice so far as supporting evidence is concerned, since the religious references in both plays have been found flippant, daring, offensive, amusing, profound, and ironic—all at the whim of the individual critic who interprets them. So generalizations about such passages had better be qualified by the recognition that diversity of subject does, in fact, give diversity of signification. On the one hand, in a play like *Volpone*, traditional religious and moral values clearly and consistently underline the unquestionable deficiencies of the comic world projected. On the other hand, it is very difficult to understand precisely in what way a sexual joke involving casual references to Lent and Easter 'mirrors ironic themes of the fall, of grace, of redemption', that are 'at the heart' of *The Man of Mode*.[18] Seek though one may, it is hard to find anything tangible concerning any grace or fall in Etherege's comedy. Dorimant and Harriet both play the game of love with skill and success; they best all their other opponents, and they finally arrange a return engagement with each other in the country. Where does either of them fall? Where, specifically, does either of them show any theological 'grace'? Where is their triumph seriously challenged? In fact and in context, they conspicuously emerge as this particular play's winners, not as its losers; for they win their games within a comic world dominated by the values which they embody.

The prevailing values of Congreve's last two comedies are something else again, and ultimately, in *The Way of the World*, Congreve holds the values of *The Man of Mode* up to question. On a technical level, however, Congreve, like Etherege, exploits the duplicities and dualities of Restoration society for differing comic purposes throughout his career. The fun of *The Double Dealer* comes from watching Maskwell's manipulations, manœuvrings, and improvisations. Maskwell is a kind of comic Richard III, who gleefully enjoys his vices, lets the audience in on his nefarious schemes, and manages to steal the show before he gets caught by the virtuous characters. In his later comedies Congreve goes beyond making easy dramatic capital out of such a conspicuous dissembler and shows us the comic difficulties of understanding, of knowledge, of certainty, which are bound to arise in a world where a mask might prove preferable to the face behind it, and where virtuous and vicious characters alike are such experts in the art of acting that it is nearly impossible to determine what motives lie behind the masks they wear.

Love for Love is full of talk about dissembling. 'Never let us know one another better;' says Angelica, 'for the Pleasure of a Masquerade is done, when we come to shew Faces' (IV. i. 789–90). At the moment she says this, Angelica is counterfeiting indifference to Valentine, who has been counterfeiting madness. Later in the play, Angelica's statement proves literally true so far

---

[18] See W. B. Carnochan, ed., *The Man of Mode* (Lincoln, Nebr., 1966), p. xx.

as Mr. Tattle and Mrs. Frail are concerned. Tattle (disguised as Valentine disguised as a friar) and Mrs. Frail (disguised as Angelica disguised as a nun) discover that the pleasure of their masquerade is indeed over when they show their faces and learn, to their alarm, that they have married each other. Marriage inevitably brings with it certain knowledge of the face behind the mask, and this knowledge frequently brings disillusionment. Thus Angelica and Valentine do their best to learn the truth in advance of the marriage ceremony. Angelica, for instance, justifies her refusal to agree with Valentine that 'the Comedy draws toward an end' and they should 'think of leaving acting' and be themselves, because she remains in doubt about his motives: 'I thought your love of me had caus'd this Transport in your Soul; which, it seems, you only counterfeited, for mercenary Ends, and sordid Interest' (IV. i. 722–4). Because Valentine has dissembled to her, Angelica plays him 'Trick for Trick' and keeps on counterfeiting indifference to him. Therefore, in the final scene she feels obliged to reassure Valentine that her newly displayed love is genuine: 'I have done dissembling now, *Valentine*; and if that Coldness which I have always worn before you, should turn to an extream Fondness, you must not suspect it' (V. i. 605–7).

Such a reassurance is not superfluous in the comic world of *Love for Love*, where 'All well-bred Persons Lie' (II. i. 610–11). Sometimes circumstances force them to lie. Almost the only way Valentine can hold his inheritance for a time, and certainly the only way he can be free to tell the truth,[19] is by feigning madness. 'Mad' is Congreve's own favourite adjective for the world of this comedy. Valentine's madness appears to be a 'contagious frenzy' and practically every character in the play appears mad to some other character. The blunt Ben argues that it is mad to dissemble, but Valentine finds that his repeated insistence on telling the truth is the surest way to convince everyone of his madness. Given this sort of world, Congreve concludes that dissembling

---

[19] See Congreve, *Amendments to Mr. Collier's . . . Citations*, p. 56: 'A third use of this pretended madness is, that it gives a Liberty to Satire; and authorises a Bluntness, which would otherwise have been a Breach in the Manners of the Character.'

is neither good nor bad, neither right nor wrong, in and of itself, but that the reasons for dissembling may be good or bad ones. Thus, though his heroine rarely speaks what she thinks—her words frequently contradict her thoughts, and her actions sometimes contradict her words—Angelica's caution is shown to be justified, given her comic situation and Valentine's attempt to trick her (IV. i. 8-11).

In both its method and its meaning, the comic organization of *Love for Love* differs from the organization of *The Man of Mode* in several revealing ways. Where Etherege's hero and heroine generally manage to control their comic situations, Congreve's comic situation itself controls Valentine and (to a lesser degree) Angelica until the very last scene. Also, in *Love for Love* their motives for dissembling rather than their success in dissembling finally determine the rewards and punishments distributed to the various characters in the end. In *The Man of Mode* the motivation of the major characters is a kind of *donnée*—all the ladies, for instance, set out to get Dorimant, while Dorimant is out to get them first. And the prizes in Etherege's comedy go to the characters who attain, by surest means, the goals at which they aim. In Congreve's comedy, 'love for love allows'. All Valentine's frantic efforts to win Angelica and save his inheritance are unsuccessful. All his calculations fail. But his generous concern for Angelica's happiness finally wins him both love and wealth since, without realizing it, Valentine passes Angelica's final examination with flying colours. Conversely, Angelica's dissembling and calculations pay off when she wins the certain knowledge of Valentine's genuine and unselfish love. In neat contrast, the treacherous and mercenary schemes of Mrs. Frail and Tattle appropriately boomerang, and they get trick for trick. Congreve's first-class characters, with their first-class motives, deserve and therefore win each other. His second-class characters, with their meaner motives, also get—and deserve—each other. But Congreve's poetic justice takes up only a few minutes of this comedy. The play's sustained and primary emphasis is not on poetic justice, and certainly not on providential justice. Its sustained emphasis is on 'counterfeited Shapes', on the disguises of love, and on the variety of comic masks of madness which Valentine describes (IV. i. 700–1). The comedy shows us the problems of determining how to act, when to act, and when to leave off acting. It shows us the dilemmas which arise from the fact that it is almost impossible to know, with certainty, how others will act, why they are acting, or indeed when they are acting. And the play asks whether there is, in truth, any 'effectual Difference between continued Affectation and Reality' (III. i. 40–1). The baffled Valentine, for instance, has no tangible evidence that Angelica's feigned indifference is not genuine indifference until the last scene. The whole comic action is a whirligig of similar dilemmas. And while Ben, who is unable to act at all, makes a fine fool of himself, so does Sir Sampson, who chooses the wrong part and is warned against overacting it: 'Have a care, and don't over-act your Part—If you remember, the strongest *Sampson* of your Name, pull'd an old House over his Head at last' (V. i. 157–9). Later, of course, this bit of Biblical history proves prophetic of Sir Sampson's comic defeat. But if Congreve toys with typology here, he does it in the same way that he plays with Old Foresight's astrological lore, and he does it for the same purpose—to amuse.

Indeed, comic prophecies, oracles, *doubles entendres*, tricks, and puzzles pervade this play. Here is Valentine's account of the riddle that Angelica's behaviour represents:

Valentine. From a Riddle, you can expect nothing but a Riddle. There's my Instruction, and the Moral of my Lesson.

Re-enter Jeremy.

Jeremy. What, is the Lady gone again, Sir? I hope you understood one another before she went.

Valentine. Understood! She is harder to be understood than a Piece of *Ægyptian* Antiquity, or an *Irish* Manuscript; you may pore till you spoil your Eyes, and not improve your Knowledge.

Jeremy. I have heard 'em say, Sir, they read hard *Hebrew* Books backwards; may be you begin to read at the wrong End.

Valentine. They say so of a Witches Pray'r, and Dreams and *Dutch* Almanacks are to be understood by contraries. But there's Regularity and Method in that; she is a Medal without a Reverse or Inscription; for Indifference has both sides alike. Yet while she does not seem to

hate me, I will pursue her, and know her if it be possible, in spight of
the Opinion of my Satirical Friend, *Scandal*, who says,

> That Women are like Tricks by slight of Hand,
> Which, to admire, we should not understand.

(iv. i. 795–816)

This exchange between Valentine and Jeremy seems to me to
bring us closer to the essence of the action, the intellectual content, and the language of *Love for Love* than all its scattered religious
allusions put together.[20] And finally, Angelica herself, a human
personality which is masked until it chooses to let its true nature
be known—and not providential justice—proves to be the minis-
tering angel who distributes this play's rewards and retribution:
'Well, Madam, You have done Exemplary Justice, in punishing an
inhumane Father, and rewarding a Faithful Lover' (v. i. 619–21).
But if Angelica is something like an angel in her mysteriousness
and in her administration of exemplary justice, she is not brought
out on the stage for the purposes of supernatural allegory.
She is brought out on the stage to represent, and to experience
for herself, the comic dilemmas (or, if we must have high seriousness, the essential mysteries) inherent in the presentation of self
and the understanding of others. And these specifically human
dilemmas are the ideal subjects for superb social comedy with
enduring validity. For they are dilemmas which provide us with
comedy (and mystery) enough, both behind the footlights of the
Restoration theatre and out in the common daylight of ordinary
social experience.[21] It therefore seems unnecessary to replace this
play's dramatic realities (and its dramatic mysteries) with the fiction of a 'Providential justice' which 'governs all human affairs'—

---

[20] Contrast the (comparatively) simpler ambiguities of Wycherley's *Country
Wife*, which are all based on puns and dramatic extensions of puns: there is the
essential pun implied in Horner's name; constant verbal play on the words
'Horner' and 'Honour' which establish all possible comic relationships between
them; the sustained *double entendre* of the china scene; insistence on the double
meanings involved in Margery's disguise as a boy and Horner's reputation for
impotence; and constant references to the double identity of the actor. All these
features of Wycherley's play combine to create (in the words which Angell Day
used to define the pun) 'a pleasant kind of collusion in significations divers'.

[21] See Erving Goffman, *The Presentation of Self in Everyday Life* (London, 1969).

a fiction which will not bear close scrutiny in the specific context of *Love for Love* or in our everyday experience of the world which Congreve's comedy reflects. And Congreve's final comic image of the way of the world is, if anything, even more explicitly insistent upon truth to its model than *Love for Love*.

Written after Collier's attack on the immorality and profaneness of the stage, and intended as a kind of dramatic answer to Collier,[22] *The Way of the World* is a truly moral play, though its morality is secular and requires no reinforcement from any supernatural frame of reference, or from any cluster of religious allusions. Very obviously, its hero and its heroine are more honourable than their adversaries, and their virtue is rewarded in the end. But certain qualities which might seem at odds with pure, unmitigated virtue are also involved in their comic triumph. In fact, their shrewd calculations and extreme caution are even more explicitly responsible for their success than is their good behaviour. For while they are, in the last analysis, on the side of the angels, Mirabell and Millamant are just as conniving, contriving, and canny as Dorimant and Harriet. They have to be in order to beat Fainall and Marwood at their own game. Congreve's elegant comedy is thus a good deal more cynical and a great deal more realistic than any beautifully carved image of providential justice ever could be, and the critical argument whereby 'the Providential ordering of event in the play has been made totally tacit and utterly implicit, completely to be understood from what happens and the way it happens, rather than from any overt allusions or appeals to Providence'[23] soars as high above and as far away from the text as it is possible for a critical pursuit of phantoms to go. The text itself forces us right back down to earth, since it is rooted in truth concerning things as they are, and thus it remains completely independent of any critical or theological idealisms concerning things as they might be. In fact, whether we like it or not, this comedy effectively shows us how much scheming, artifice, and enlightened self-interest are inherent in human efforts

---

[22] See Herbert Davis, *The Complete Plays of William Congreve*, p. 386.
[23] Aubrey Williams, 'Poetical Justice, the Contrivances of Providence, and the Works of William Congreve', p. 562.

to cope, whether honourably or dishonourably, with everyday personal relationships. John Downes thought *The Way of the World* failed because it was too keen a satire, and indeed the comedy is a degree or two more cynical in its outlook than *Love for Love*, where Valentine's sheer perseverance in loving Angelica saw him safely through the social labyrinth. For Mirabell, steadfast love is not enough. Before he can claim his Millamant and the fortune which goes with her, Mirabell must set a very clever comic Machiavel to school. Indeed, this comedy as a whole insists that if its hero and heroine are ever to transcend the 'ways of wedlock and this world' which are embodied in Fainall and Marwood, they first have to find some way to master them. But it is impossible to talk any further about Congreve's message without fuller reference to his dramatic medium, since (rather like *Measure for Measure*) Congreve's comic masterpiece poses some perplexing problems for its audience.

6 'Offending against decorums': the reflection of social experience in *The Way of the World*

> Who is the counterfeit's example? His original.   ROCHESTER
>
> Tell me if Congreve's fools are fools indeed?   POPE
>
> To understand the World, and to like it, are two things not easily to be reconciled. . . . It is the fools and the knaves that make the wheels of the World turn. They *are* the World; those few who have sense or honesty sneak up and down single, but never go in herds.
>
> HALIFAX

MODERN critics have disagreed about the dramatic emphasis of Congreve's last comedy, but they are in complete agreement about its excellence. Almost everyone who writes about the play in any detail concludes that *The Way of the World* is the greatest comedy of its genre. And certainly, like its heroine, Congreve's masterpiece makes even its most attractive rivals look either too flashy or too pale by comparison. Nevertheless, the consistently favourable critical verdict on this play represents an interesting paradox, since *The Way of the World* receives and deserves its acclaim in spite of (or perhaps even because of) dramatic problems which in another play would be odious. Indeed, when Mirabell pays his famous tribute to Millamant, he gives us a strikingly accurate account of the critical response evoked by the comedy itself:

I like her with all her Faults; nay, like her for her Faults. Her Follies are so natural, or so artful, that they become her; and those Affectations which in another Woman wou'd be odious, serve but to make her more agreeable. I'll tell thee, *Fainall*, she once us'd me with that Insolence, that in Revenge I took her to pieces; sifted her and separated her Failings; I study'd 'em, and got 'em by rote. The Catalogue was so large, that I was not without hopes, one Day or other to hate her heartily: To which end I so us'd my self to think of 'em, that at length, contrary to my Design and Expectation, they gave me every Hour less and less disturbance; 'till in a few Days it became habitual to me, to remember 'em without being displeas'd.

(I. i. 159–74)

In *The Way of the World* Congreve uses his admirers with an insolence comparable to Millamant's. He virtually challenges us to catalogue the obvious faults of his comedy, and then he forces us to conclude that if we like his masterpiece at all, we necessarily like it with all its faults. Furthermore, though its failings seem unforgivable on a first reading, upon familiarity they seem so natural, or so artful, that in the final analysis they serve but to make the play more agreeable. Still, the fact remains that on first introduction *The Way of the World* confronts us with a large catalogue of dramatic frailties, including an incomprehensible plot, a baffling network of family relationships, a villain who is easily confused with the hero, and an ambiguous moral attitude towards the hero himself. It is only after we study the play, after we take it to pieces, sift it, and separate its failings, that we find that its frailties give us less and less disturbance, and ultimately conclude that we like it with its faults, nay, even like it for its faults.

Four major problems arise in the opening scenes of *The Way of the World*. These problems are closely related, since they all serve to create confusion on the part of the audience. First, the plot is obscure from the outset. 'Some Plot we think he has', says the Prologue, but its metre might reflect a certain sly scepticism in this regard. And surely when we learn at the end that Mirabell has held Fainall's purse-strings from the very beginning, we may well ask exactly what *was* the plot of this comedy. Secondly, it is quite impossible to unravel the snarl of family relationships which are described to Mirabell (and introduced to us) in the first scene: '[Sir Wilfull] is half Brother to this *Witwoud* by a former Wife, who was Sister to my Lady *Wishfort*, my Wife's Mother. If you marry *Millamant* you must call Cousins too' (I. i. 192–5). Now if this laughably baffling genealogical table is not deliberately laughable and deliberately baffling, then Congreve's reputation

as a major comic playwright had better be revised post-haste.
In fact, this catalogue of kinship goes out of its way to break every
one of the laws governing exposition that were neatly codified
in a book about *The Whole Art of the Stage* which Congreve may
have studied carefully earlier in his career. According to the rules,
all 'Dramatick Narrations' should 'enter into the Composition of
the Dramatick Poem, for two ends, either to make it clear and
intelligible, or to adorn and set it out'. Clarity is the main goal,
and playwrights should avoid falling into errors which defeat
this purpose:

> The first [of these errors] is, when his Narration is obscure, and
> loaded with circumstances hard for the Audience to retain distinctly;
> such are *Genealogical* ones . . . or a great number of Names, with
> a Chain of actions embroyl'd one in another; for the Spectator will
> not give himself the trouble to observe and retain all these different
> *Idæa's*, he coming to the Stage only for his pleasure, and in the mean
> time for want of remembring all this, he remains in the dark as to the
> rest of the Play, and is disgusted for all the time he stays.[1]

Congreve not only violates these rules, his fantastically complicated genealogical table calls comic attention to his violation of
them. Thus we had best conclude that the genealogical history
is deliberately designed to create a state of comic confusion—
a state which is inhabited by the play's audience as well as by its
characters. Otherwise we must conclude that it is our critical
duty to point out the grievous error of Congreve's ways, and go
on to correct his mistakes for him. But an account of the disaster
that occurred when the 1969 production at the Old Vic attempted
to clarify the genealogical relationships which Congreve so conspicuously confused grimly warns us either to take the play as it
stands or else leave it alone. According to *The Observer* review
(4 May 1969),

> The main virtue of the new National Theatre revival is that, with
> the help of a family tree in the programme, it enables one to arrive at

---

[1] François Hédelin, *The Whole Art of the Stage* (London, 1684), Book iii,
pp. 16–17. For Congreve's possible use of Hédelin in *The Old Batchelor* see
Herbert Davis, *The Complete Plays of William Congreve*, p. 4. Congreve had a copy
of the original French edition of 1657, and also of the English translation of 1684.

[the play's] chronicle of sexual and financial adventurism ... Yet something has gone wrong. . . . Somehow the most exquisitely written comedy in English has gone coarse and leaden. The marvellous verbal sallies and fantasy too often miss fire. Instead of gaining, as you'd expect, in clarity and masterful lightness, it bogs down in tortuous explanation and intrigue.

And the review then outlines the weird perversion of Congreve's comedy which resulted from this effort to achieve genealogical clarity:

Sometime during Stuart England's upheavals, a wealthy gentleman left a fortune of some £36,000 between his three daughters, whom he had married into the baronetage. The two older girls also bore only daughters, so that by the end of the century a matriarchy of money had grown up: a house of rich, strong-willed women who tended to outlive their husbands, its purse-strings held by the surviving eldest sister, a widowed bluestocking of greater sexual appetite than sense.

To protect the family inheritance against the fortune hunters buzzing about it, the old lady surrounded herself with women friends and half-men, and tried to force a match between her niece and nephew, the youngest sister's countrified son. But the citadel had been infiltrated. Her son-in-law, uncovering an old affair between her daughter and one of the fortune-hunters, threatened public scandal unless given control of the family fortune. Luckily (so to speak) the girl had already deeded her share to her lover, and by letting him marry the niece the dynasty secured itself a male protector at the cost of its independence. Which, children, is how Mirabell and Millamant became the most famous lovers in Restoration comedy.

If this trivial, gross, and dull chronicle is the price we must pay for a clarification of the Wishfort-Witwoud family tree, then the price is simply too high. Certainly this tedious footnote on English social and economic history has nothing in common with Congreve's greatest comedy. On the other hand, if we start out with the assumption that Congreve's play is deliberately designed to reflect a world of confused social and personal relationships, we can accept its comic genealogical table without sacrificing the rest of the play in order to clarify it. We can also observe, without undue dismay, that the third problem posed by the play—the initial problem of distinguishing between its hero and its villain—

is yet another dramatic means of introducing us into a comic world where social and personal relationships are confused, and confusing.

Over the years, everybody has noticed that the opening scenes of *The Way of the World* make it very difficult to pinpoint the essential difference between Mirabell and Fainall. It has also been evident to everyone that even the most conspicuous fools in this comedy have a surprising number of witty lines. Dedicating *The Way of the World* to the Earl of Montague, Congreve himself discusses these specific features of the play. Congreve describes *The Way of the World* as an experimental comedy in which he adopted methods of organization new to him and new to Restoration comedy in order to portray characters who are ridiculous not because of their natural follies, but because of their affected wit. His distinction between 'True Wit', and 'Wit, which at the same time that it is affected, is also false', apparently was too subtle for certain members of the audience: 'For this Play had been Acted two or three Days, before some . . . hasty Judges cou'd find the leisure to distinguish betwixt the Character of a *Witwoud* and a *Truewit*.' At first glance this failure on the part of the audience might appear puzzling, since it is not all that difficult to spot the difference between Mirabell and Witwoud himself. But Congreve's major distinction between Fainall's feigned wit and the genuine wit of Mirabell does create problems. Probably the best gloss on his distinction between these characters appears in Congreve's answer of 1698 to Collier, where he explicitly analyses the relationship between Wit and Understanding:

Wit is at best but the *Sign* to good understanding; it is hung out to recommend the Entertainment which may be found within: And it is very well when the Invitation can be made good. As the outward form of Godliness is Hypocrisie, which very often conceals Irreligion and Immorality; so is Wit also very often an Hypocrisie, a Superficies glaz'd upon false Judgment, a good Face set on a bad Understanding.[2]

[2] Congreve, *Amendments of Mr. Collier's False and Imperfect Citations* (1698), p. 95. And according to George Savile, first Marquess of Halifax, 'A man that hath true wit will have honour too, not only to adorn, but to support it' (*Miscellaneous Thoughts and Reflections*).

To draw the fine line between Mirabell's wit, which reflects true judgement, and Fainall's wit, which is a 'Superficies glaz'd upon false Judgment', Congreve first emphasizes the fact that their outward manifestations may be very similar indeed. Then, after he has stressed their superficial similarity, Congreve shows us the very differing motives and the differing kinds of judgement which may hide behind the 'Sign' of wit. Thus, though their names instruct us to expect a major distinction between Fainall and Mirabell, Congreve's introduction of the two characters reveals that wit's counterfeit may be such a good copy of its original that it takes close scrutiny to recognize the essential difference between them, that is, the vast difference in value behind them. Therefore, while Fainall's nefarious motives, like Mirabell's honourable motives, become evident enough as the play develops, in their first encounters the motives of both characters lie hidden from us by the playwright himself. And here again we find Congreve breaking contemporary rules governing a playwright's treatment of his audience. According to contemporary dramatic decorums, 'the Poet must bring no Actor upon the Stage that is not known to the Spectators as soon as he appears, and that not only as to his Name and Person, but also as to the Sentiments he brings upon the Stage, else the Spectator will be puzzled, and the Poets fine Discourses will be lost, because the Audience will not know how to apply them.'[3] As we shall see in a subsequent discussion of the play's language, it is certainly true that we do not know, that we cannot know, exactly how to apply the fine discourses between Fainall and Mirabell which introduce us to the Byzantine intrigues of *The Way of the World*.

The fourth problem created by the comedy is a directly related one, since Congreve's initial presentation of Fainall and Mirabell brings with it the inevitable bone of critical contention concerning the morality, immorality, or amorality of the play's dramatic assumptions. 'In their haste to approve of Mirabell,' John Wain complains, 'some critics have simply not noticed what a cad he is.' As Wain points out, the play makes it evident that Mirabell and Fainall alike have given Mrs. Fainall a very bad time.

[3] Hédelin, *The Whole Art of the Stage*, iii, p. 5.

If the lady is unhappily married to the villain, the hero himself is directly responsible for her plight. Mirabell, in John Wain's words, 'pushed Mrs. Fainall into a marriage of hell, to suit his own convenience'. And is this any way for a hero to treat a lady? Though Mirabell is 'the *hero*' and thus 'we are supposed to care whether he is happy or not', given his cynical treatment of Mrs. Fainall, Mr. Wain concludes that it is 'no wonder Lamb could only defend these plays by saying that they were simply aesthetic patterns with no humanity involved at all'.[4] Thus, at the same time that this comedy creates dramatic confusion it also creates genuine moral confusion. For the questions which John Wain raises are questions explicitly raised by the play itself.

To illustrate the moral dilemmas posed by *The Way of the World* we need only contrast the amoral clarities of *The Man of Mode*. Throughout his comedy, Etherege leaves Dorimant wide open to attacks by preachers and prudes. But by doing so, he deftly defies us, while he dares us, to launch such attacks against his gilded lover, since the minute we start deploring Dorimant's wicked ways we find ourselves sounding as priggish as Jeremy Collier. Etherege equally effectively eliminates moral criteria from our judgements of his other characters. We do not damn Mrs. Loveit or Bellinda because they have committed fornication with Dorimant, we simply recognize that by doing so they threw away their trump cards in the game of love. Furthermore (as we have seen) Etherege gives us a set of very explicit, completely amoral criteria by which to judge his characters (skill in the game of love, expertise in the art of acting, sang-froid, and elegance), all of which may manifest themselves in moral and immoral characters alike. Thus when he is evaluated by the play's own standards, Dorimant emerges as a 'Fine Gentleman', as the very model of a modern libertine, and he held the stage as such for 'fifty years together'. Congreve takes us in the opposite direction. By giving both his hero and his villain equally abundant shares of the elegance, intelligence, and witty lines that Etherege gives to Dorimant, Congreve effectively eliminates these social and dramatic

---

[4] John Wain, 'Restoration Comedy and its Modern Critics', *Preliminary Essays* (London, 1957), p. 21.

advantages as criteria by which we can distinguish between Mirabell and Fainall. Since they are equally matched so far as the outward signs of 'wit' are concerned, the ultimate distinction between them becomes a moral distinction based on their motives. But herein lies the moral dilemma that is posed by this comedy. Whereas no character in *The Man of Mode* is held up to clear moral judgement, Congreve subjects Fainall to precisely this kind of judgement. Simultaneously, he presents Mirabell as Fainall's dramatic antithesis, as the comic hero who is opposed to the comic villain. But then Congreve blurs the clarity of his moral distinction between them and tells us that Mirabell himself was guilty of some outrageous double dealing when he married off his mistress to a known cad because they feared she was pregnant and needed to fix the name of father to their child. Without any authorial comment whatsoever, the audience is left to interpret the following discussion of Mrs. Fainall's marriage:

> *Mirabell.* You shou'd have just so much disgust for your Husband, as may be sufficient to make you relish your Lover.
> *Mrs. Fainall.* You have been the cause that I have lov'd without Bounds, and wou'd you set Limits to that Aversion, of which you have been the occasion? Why did you make me marry this Man?
> *Mirabell.* Why do we daily commit disagreeable and dangerous Actions? To save that Idol Reputation. If the familiarities of our Loves had produc'd that Consequence, of which you were apprehensive, where could you have fix'd a Father's Name with Credit, but on a Husband? I knew *Fainall* to be a Man lavish of his Morals, an interested and professing Friend, a false and designing Lover; yet one whose Wit and outward fair Behaviour have gain'd a Reputation with the Town, enough to make that Woman stand excus'd, who has suffer'd herself to be won by his Addresses. A better Man ought not to have been sacrific'd to the Occasion; a worse had not answer'd to the Purpose. When you are weary of him, you know your Remedy.
>
> (II. i. 258–77)

Congreve does not influence his audience to respond to this situation in any specific way. Mrs. Fainall's unhappy marriage is never the target for scornful laughter, nor is it the subject of righteous indignation. Congreve certainly does not present this marriage as a comic joke comparable to the marriage that Jeremy arranged between Mrs. Frail and Tattle, but he never once implies that Mirabell himself should have married Mrs. Fainall. Probably the Fainall *mariage de convenance* simply serves to illustrate a rather common way of wedlock, given Congeve's post-lapsarian world. Mrs. Fainall needed a husband. Fainall needed her money. Mirabell needed a way out. Certainly the whole situation accurately reflects the simple fact that the social world requires decent and wicked people alike to make compromises with its demands in order to survive within it. When their human frailties and passions get them into trouble, 'the world' very frequently forces even its nicest inhabitants to find some socially acceptable (though personally repellent) way out of it. In fact, this whole play insists that its characters, good and bad alike, come to terms with their world. It insists that they put up with it, that they make the best of it: and Congreve's emphasis on accommodation will get more discussion later. But so far as Mirabell's own behaviour towards Mrs. Fainall is concerned, Congreve (like Fielding in *Tom Jones*) may be insisting that we should not condemn a character as a bad one because he is not a perfectly good one.

Defending his earlier comic hero, Valentine, against Collier's attack, Congreve argues that 'the Character is a mix'd Character; his Faults are fewer than his good Qualities; and, as the World goes, he may pass well enough for the best Character in a Comedy; where even the best must be shewn to have Faults, that the best Spectators may be warn'd not to think too well of themselves.'[5] Certainly, in spite of all its theorizing about scourging the vices and follies of its time, social comedy itself usually permits us to respond to its characters with a goodly measure of tolerance. It permits us to smile at, and thereby encourages us to accept, the social scene which it portrays. And it very seldom presumes to distribute writs of eternal salvation or damnation to its characters. This may be a very good thing. For if, in art or in life, we

[5] Congreve, *Amendments of Mr. Collier's False and Imperfect Citations*, pp. 89–90. Like Collier, John Wain asks the question, 'What about Valentine's [illegitimate] child?' (*Preliminary Essays*, p. 20).

continually had to issue ultimate judgements, both art and life would be intolerable, and so would we. In fact, the middle range of judgement which governs social comedy is our most common range of judgement, given our everyday experience with a fallen world. For instance, we can enjoy Congreve's plays without shuddering in horror at the historical evidence that he left his money to the young Duchess of Marlborough in order to assure that their daughter would discreetly inherit it. Similar things happen so frequently that most people manage to forgive them, just as Mrs. Fainall herself clearly forgives Mirabell and even helps him to court Millamant. In fact, Mr. Wain himself admits that Congreve's presentation of the Fainall marriage involves 'admirable realism'. And maybe (from one point of view at least) its 'admirable realism' is its true justification. From a related point of view (my own point of view) the situation makes it patently unfair for us to cast too many stones at Fainall without throwing a few at Mrs. Fainall and Mirabell as well. So perhaps the final solution is simply not to cast any stones at all, but rather to recognize the social truths which these characters and their situation exhibit before us. This interpretation obviously begs the moral question instead of answering it. But perhaps it is legitimate for a comedy to raise, then beg, moral questions if it does so in order to direct its appeal from any artificial aesthetic or moral structures back towards ordinary experience, back towards the manifold, everyday problems to which there may not be any ideally happy solution (or any ideally moral solution) either available to, or fair to, all the people involved. 'As the world goes', then, Mirabell may pass well enough for the best character in his comedy. And maybe his true moral purpose is to remind us all not to think too highly of ourselves. Obviously all this is sheer speculation, and as such it is inconclusive; but the fact that inconclusive speculation is aroused by the dialogue between Mirabell and Mrs. Fainall itself illustrates an essential difference between *The Way of the World* and other famous comedies of its kind. In another Restoration comedy (in *The Man of Mode*, for instance) we would know —the author would let us know—precisely what attitude we should adopt towards this sort of encounter between a rakish hero and his discarded mistress. But Mirabell is not a conventional rake, Mrs. Fainall is not a conventional discarded mistress, and *The Way of the World* is not a conventional Restoration comedy.

Indeed, turning from a more typical comedy of this period, turning from, say, *Love for Love*, to *The Way of the World* can only be compared to turning from *The Malcontent* to *Measure for Measure*, or from an excellent 'well-made' play to *The Seagull*. There are generic similarities, but in the long run they only serve to enhance the differences between such plays. In contrast to *The Way of the World*, *Love for Love* creates difficulties only for its characters; never for its audience. The plot is clear. Valentine, who loves Angelica, has been disinherited, and after a series of comic complications he gets his inheritance back and wins the heroine. There is no question in this comedy whether Congreve's fools are fools indeed. They are. The hero and heroine are surrounded by a gallery of familiar comic types: a country girl who wants to learn city ways, a fop, a boor, two old fools, etc.[6] These characters never deviate from established patterns of comic behaviour, and our responses to them, conditioned from their first entrances, never vary. Like characters in Roman comedy, or in Molière's plays, the comic types of *Love for Love* always behave as we expect them to, and each time they conform to our expectations we laugh with recognition.[7] The central aim of this popular

[6] On Congreve's use of traditional types see Herbert Davis, *The Complete Plays of William Congreve*, pp. 11–12, 206.

[7] See Georges Poulet's discussion of Molière's own account of this mode of comic presentation in *Studies in Human Time*, tr. Elliott Coleman (Baltimore, Md., 1956), pp. 103–4. According to Molière, 'The excessive ridicule of the manners of Panulphe makes it certain that every time they are presented to the spectator on some other occasion they will assuredly seem to him ridiculous. . . . The soul, naturally avid of joy, will necessarily be delighted at the first sight of things that it once conceived as extremely ridiculous, and *will renew in itself the idea of the very lively pleasure it tasted that first time*.' Therefore, says Poulet, 'each time we notice a new comic manifestation of character, "we shall be first of all struck by the memory of that first time", and this memory, mingling itself with the present occasion, will "fuse the two occasions into one".' And thus, Poulet concludes, 'to the objective repetition of the course of passion there is joined the subjective repetition of the feeling it provokes in us. The character repeats himself and we begin to laugh again, and in beginning to laugh again we accord to him once more the freshness of actuality.'

mode of comic presentation is cumulative laughter—a single response which grows in intensity through repetition, so that the twentieth time a character says 'y'gad' or 'very interesting' is funnier than the tenth time he said it. So while the action of *Love for Love* may surprise us, Old Foresight, Ben, and Sir Sampson do not surprise us. And however baffled, boorish, bombastic, or befuddled the individual characters in *Love for Love* may be, we in the audience remain superior and secure in our possession of privileged information concerning them. We are fully aware of all their intentions and pretensions. We are thus spared the dilemmas involved in determining motives, we are safe from the dangers of attributing false motives, and we are free from the uncertainties about other people which confront us in ordinary life, and which confront Valentine and Angelica up there on the stage.

In *The Way of the World* Congreve deliberately confronts his audience with precisely the same dilemmas faced by his characters. The contrasts to his mode of presentation in *Love for Love* make it even more evident that in the opening scenes of his last comedy Congreve departs from his previous practice to lead us into a comic world where we ourselves are not sure just what is going on, where we are uncertain who may be related to or in love with whom, and where we wonder whether the people we meet are honourable or dishonourable. Such insecure responses are unusual responses to the expository scenes of a Restoration comedy, but they certainly are familiar enough in ordinary social experience. Reading or seeing *The Way of the World* for the first time, one feels like an outsider at a smart cocktail party who overhears snatches of conversation, the implications of which he does not fully understand ('When you are weary of him, you know your remedy'); who classifies the guests in certain ways only to learn later that his initial classifications were all wrong, that Miss Y, who he had decided was in love with Mr. X, is actually the mistress of Mr. Z, or that the witty and elegant man who seemed so amusing is a vicious cad. Obviously this sort of gradual process of discovery is not the usual expository way of Restoration comedy. We learn all we need to know about the natures of Dorimant, Loveit, Ben, Horner, and Lady Fidget in the first five minutes of our acquaintance with them. But a continuing process of discovery is the usual way of the social world we all live in.

In his title, Congreve insists that he imitates life, but his peculiar method of imitating social life in *The Way of the World* is more frequently encountered in the novel, or in modern drama (in Henry James, Proust, or Chekhov) than in Restoration comedy. In this play characters who only gradually reveal their true natures to us, who only gradually reveal their true attitudes towards each other, are set off against other characters (Witwoud, Petulant, Lady Wishfort) who continue to behave in accord with our first impressions of them. And rather like Lady Wishfort herself, we in the audience frequently must modify our own original reactions to several characters and situations. Sir Wilfull, whom everybody automatically classifies as a stock boor from the country who is ruder than Gothic, turns up on the side of the Truewits in the end. Millamant, the proud and ostensibly heartless heroine, gradually reveals a certain vulnerability and fear. Fainall's great elegance and dry wit prove to be the masks of malice. At first glance, Mrs. Fainall appears identical to Marwood, a bitter and jealous woman who has been scorned, but she later becomes a very sympathetic figure. And our final responses to such characters are cumulative in a peculiar way, since Congreve gives us a series of partial perspectives on them that combine in a comprehensive response which frequently assimilates the previous ones. For instance, our appreciation of Sir Wilfull's generosity does not preclude continuing laughter at his boorishness. Similarly, enjoyment of Fainall's witty cynicism remains even when he behaves with extreme cruelty, and our pity for Lady Wishfort's serious predicament does not stop our laughter at her bombastic discomfiture:

Lady Wishfort. This is most inhumanly Savage; exceeding the Barbarity of a *Muscovite* Husband.

Fainall. I learn'd it from his *Czarish* Majestie's Retinue, in a Winter Evenings Conference over Brandy and Pepper, amongst other secrets of Matrimony and Policy, as they are at present Practis'd in the *Northern* Hemisphere.

(v. i. 271–6)

Thus where other Restoration comedies frequently simplify audience responses for the sake of comic intensity (perhaps by eliminating sympathy for their comic targets), Congreve complicates our responses throughout *The Way of the World*. And our complicated, sometimes uncertain, responses are the clear result of the play's form and the accurate reflection of its meaning, given a world where our responses to people and situations inevitably grow more complex when more is known about them. Since the plot hardly moves at all, the movements of the play really are the progressive revelations of character, the movements of the characters into new relationships with each other, and the movements of our own progressive understanding of the various characters and their situations. All this is an elaborate way of saying that Congreve first presents us with apparently simple surfaces, with stock types and situations, and then he takes us beneath the surfaces and behind the masks. What, this play asks, may hide behind the stereotypes of comic and social forms? And when dramatic and social forms that once served to reveal character have become dramatic and social ends in themselves, why can they not serve equally well to conceal character? Congreve's last comedy is all about the forms of language and manners, about the forms of wit. It is a graceful, elegant, unsentimental, comic, and incisive exhibition of what these forms may conceal and what they may reveal. And this play's extraordinary way of first defining its own form as that of a typical Restoration comedy, and then proceeding to escape from its own definition, contributes both to its success and to its difficulty. For when it sets the norms and forms of contemporary drama and contemporary society against each other, *The Way of the World* ceases to be even a typical Congreve comedy. It was not what his own audience expected. There is no Miss Prue, no Tattle, no Ben. Motives, rather than cleverness, define true wit. Indeed, the formulas of witty language prove to be of no help at all, since (precisely because they are formulas) just about anybody can master them. A Fainall can speak as brilliantly as a Mirabell. Mirabell's servant can easily adopt the lingo fit for a suitor to Lady Wishfort. Similarly, the forms of manners provide no basis for distinction if a Marwood can impeccably observe the forms of friendship until it suits her convenience to abandon them. But a closer look at Congreve's presentation of his key representatives of True and False Wit, and a glance at the manners and mannerisms of Milla-mant can get us nearer to the elusive essence of this play as mani-fested in its language and in its heroine.

Until the surprising denouement of *The Way of the World*, Fainall appears to be an equal match for Mirabell. He is expert with language, perceptive, always amusing. And however hollow his wit may appear under scrutiny, it certainly sounds like the real thing.

> *Fainall.* You are a gallant Man, *Mirabell*; and tho' you may have Cruelty enough, not to satisfie a Lady's longing; you have too much Generosity, not to be tender of her Honour. Yet you speak with an Indifference which *seems to be affected*; *and confesses you are conscious* of a Negligence.
>
> *Mirabell.* You pursue the Argument with a distrust that *seems to be unaffected*, and *confesses you are conscious* of a Concern for which the Lady is more indebted to you, than your Wife.
>
> (I. i. 90–8, emphasis mine)[8]

In retrospect, when we know the play, we can admire the stiletto of Mirabell's wit as he parodies Fainall, skilfully forestalls further prying, and hints at the love affair between Fainall and Marwood. But this is possible only in retrospect, only on a second reading or viewing of the play. Likewise, an understanding of Fainall's reference to Mirabell's 'gallantry' requires information about Mar-wood's character which is withheld at this point in the action. And there are other reasons why we may be initially confused by this interchange. 'Seems to be' is equated with 'confesses you are conscious' in both speeches. To say what they think is in fact the case, each character points out what 'seems to be' the case. Mira-bell speaks with indifference, but Fainall decides that the indif-ference 'seems to be affected', and thus concludes that Mirabell is conscious of having neglected Marwood. 'What is', these speeches

---

[8] In their exchanges, Mirabell frequently gets the last word. As Dryden said, 'there may be much acuteness in a thing well said; but there is more in a quick reply.'

imply, may be the opposite of what it seems to be, or it may in fact be what it seems to be. Everything depends on whether the emotion expressed is affected or unaffected. But all this goes by like lightning. On a first reading we cannot know how to interpret this preliminary sparring because we simply do not have enough information about these characters, or about their true relationship with each other, or about their relationships with Marwood and Mrs. Fainall. We can tell that both characters are attempting to probe the truth behind the surface of appearance. We can tell that the two characters sound very much alike, and that they each claim to know a lot more about each other than we know. But, for all we know at this point in the play, the two characters are equally clever rakes who appear to be confidants. Mirabell has just described his own calculated courtship of Lady Wishfort, and Fainall makes clear his cynicism about marriage in general. Fainall's name is not even much help here, for if a character named 'Scandal' can turn out to be a pretty good friend to Valentine, a character named 'Fainall' might turn out to be simply an affected rake who is the confidant and foil of the hero. Certainly Mirabell and Fainall appear to be at one in their scorn for Witwoud. Anyway, throughout their initial encounter, the similarities between the two characters are far more evident than their differences.[9]

The parallels between Mirabell and Fainall continue into the second act, when each character walks off with a lady who is involved with the other. Fainall pairs off with his mistress, Marwood, who really loves Mirabell; and Mirabell walks with his former mistress, who is married to Fainall. Then, even as we learn of Fainall's infidelity, we learn that Mirabell himself contrived the Fainall marriage to suit his own convenience. And when Fainall admits that he married for money, we are reminded that Mirabell himself is not indifferent to Millamant's great fortune. Nevertheless, throughout the comedy, we are gradually made aware that while both characters share certain goals, and

---

[9] The original casting of the play may have contributed to the confusion between the two characters, since Betterton, who customarily played the hero, played Fainall.

certain modes of speech and behaviour, the motives and judgement behind their actions differ sharply. In retrospect, the two
characters may be seen to define opposite visions of the way of the
world from the very beginning:

> *Fainall.* For a *passionate Lover*, methinks you are a *Man* somewhat
> too *discerning* in the Failings of your Mistress.
> *Mirabell.* And for a *discerning Man*, somewhat too *passionate* a *Lover*;
> for I like her with all her Faults.
>
> (I. i. 156–60, emphasis mine)

Here Fainall accuses Mirabell of departing from the conventional
forms of courtship which would acknowledge no flaws in the
beloved. Mirabell neatly exposes the hollowness of this stereo-
typed idealism by reversing Fainall's key adjectives and nouns to
define a love which is more honest, more realistic, and far more
genuine than any courtly pose ever could be. But Mirabell's point
is not all that obvious at a glance. It is only obvious upon reflection. To illustrate the verbal subtlety that characterizes *The Way
of the World* it is helpful to contrast Mirabell's reversal of Fainall's
words with the more immediate comic effect of the same rhetorical technique ('When the words of a sentence are turned upside
down, or as I may say, repeated backward')[10] as it appears in
other plays. By giving the original placement of words to one
character, and the reversal of the same words to another, Restoration comic playwrights commonly use this device to organize
their witty repartee. For example, in *The Country Wife*, Wycherley deftly exploits the technique to expose Lady Fidget's hypocrisy
and to illustrate Horner's keen wit:

> *Lady Fidget.* . . . *affectation* makes not a Woman more odious to them
> than *Virtue*.
> *Horner.* Because your *Virtue* is your greatest *affectation*, Madam.

Wycherley's exchange of wit is funnier than Congreve's and
its impact is much more obvious. Horner's attack is direct, and
he emerges the clear verbal winner when he takes Lady Fidget's

---

[10] See John Smith's definition of *epanodos* in *The Mysterie of Rhetorique Unveil'd*
(1673), p. 90.

contraries and identifies them. And in *The Old Batchelor* Congreve explicitly calls our attention to his delicious use of this rhetorical device when he reverses the proverbial conclusion, '*Marry'd* in *haste*, we may *repent* at *leisure*', to argue that

> Some by Experience find those Words misplac'd:
> At *leisure marry'd*, they *repent* in *haste*.
> (v. i. 328–31, emphasis mine)

Amusingly, two of the key words, 'Marry'd' and 'repent', maintain the same chronological order, and this implies an unchangeable relationship between them. The significant difference lies only in the chronological 'haste' or 'leisure' of the inevitable repentance.

Clearly Mirabell's reversal of Fainall's terms 'passionate Lover' and 'discerning Man' is less overtly hilarious than either of the earlier examples of the same technique. Still, the conclusion which Mirabell reaches by this reversal comes as a striking surprise, as a kind of revelation, both to him and to us. Few passionate lovers in any period admit faults in their beloved, and hardly any of them sit down and deliberately make catalogues of the faults of their ladies. In fact, ever since Ovid, this sort of catalogue has been prescribed as one of the 'remedies of love', and Mirabell frankly admits that he originally intended to concentrate on Millamant's faults in order to cool his passion for her. But his ultimate acceptance and understanding of Millamant, with all her faults, also reveals Mirabell's full acceptance and understanding of himself.

Nevertheless, Fainall refuses to collapse in defeat: 'Marry her, marry her,' he says, 'be half as well acquainted with her Charms, as you are with her Defects, and my Life on't, you are your own Man again' (I. i. 175–7). Fainall's line is very funny, and it also rings true to the usual treatment of marriage in Restoration comedy, where sexual or emotional familiarity breeds contempt and where love is thus possible only at a safe distance. In fact, on the basis of Fainall's conclusion, and on the basis of conventional Restoration comic practice, even so perceptive a comic writer as Thackeray predicts that 'When Mirabell is sixty, having of course

divorced the first Lady Millamant, and married his friend Dori-
court's granddaughter out of the nursery—it will be his turn; and
young Belmour will make a fool of him.'[11] Of course Thackeray's
prophecy misses Congreve's distinction between the 'ways of
wedlock and this world' that are advocated by and embodied in
Fainall, and the more honest and more honourable ways that are
discovered and devised by Mirabell and Millamant. But Congreve himself always makes it very clear that in the world of this
play good marriages (like true wits) are very rare. They are the
exception rather than the rule. Fainall's own marriage of convenience is the play's example of the rule. And given the example
of wedded life set by the Fainalls, Millamant's reluctance to
'dwindle into a wife' is easy to understand.

In his famous and influential attack on Restoration comedy,
L. C. Knights summons Millamant to face severe judgement
because of her lack of 'intelligence'. But one of the witnesses that
Mr. Knights calls for the prosecution of Restoration comedy can
serve as an excellent witness in Millamant's defence.[12] In his
Advice to a Daughter, Halifax gives us an excellent perspective on
Millamant's situation, and on her artifices. Writing in the witty
style of a fatherly Mirabell, Halifax graphically describes the
dangers of the contemporary social scene: 'It is time now to lead
you out of your *House* into the *World*. A dangerous step; where
your Vertue alone will not serve you, except it is attended with
a great deal of *Prudence*: You must have *both* for your *Guard*, and
not stir without them; the Enemy is abroad, and you are sure to be
taken, if you are found straglling' (pp. 95–6). For self-protection,
his daughter (like Millamant) must remain aloof. Indeed, cautious 'Reserve' is 'a *Guard* to a *good Woman*, and a *Disguise* to

[11] Thackeray, *The English Humourists of the Eighteenth Century*, ed. George
Saintsbury (Oxford, 1908), p. 516.
[12] In 'Restoration Comedy: The Reality and the Myth', *Explorations* (London,
1946), p. 136, L. C. Knights calls George Savile, Marquess of Halifax, an 'extremely
handsome representative of his age' and uses the prose of the *Character of Charles II*
as a touchstone by which to condemn Restoration comedy as irrelevant to the best
thought of its time. But see Halifax, *The Lady's New-years Gift: or Advice to a
Daughter* (London, 1688) for a perfect gloss on *Love for Love* and *The Way of the
World*—page numbers of this edition are cited in my text.

an *ill one*. It is of so much use to both, that those ought to use it as an *Artifice*, who refuse to practice it as a *Vertue*' (p. 116). 'Reserve', when it becomes the external basis for judgement of virtue, will serve quite adequately as a cover for vice. How then does one distinguish between virtue itself and vice disguised as virtue when both involve exactly the same outward manifestations? How does one distinguish between true wit and its artful imitation? How does one distinguish between true sincerity and sincere acting? Congreve poses these problems through the prose style and characterization of a comic world where a Mirabell and a Fainall may sound, dress, and act alike. Thus Millamant quite rightly conceals her love from Mirabell and from the world. Maintain Mirabell's elegance, but pervert his motives, and you get—Fainall.

Millamant is also threatened in her dealings with women, and the song 'If there's delight in love 'tis when I see / That Heart which others bleed for bleeds for me' is a clever means of disguising her feelings and, simultaneously, exposing the prying and dangerous Marwood. It is a defence, and it certainly should not be interpreted as the summing up of Millamant's philosophy of life. In the proviso scene, Millamant explicitly insists on the substance, as opposed to the forms, of a good marriage. 'I'll not be call'd Names', she says, while one remembers the hypocritical endearments of the Fainalls. And, she goes on,

> Good *Mirabell* don't let us be familiar or fond, nor kiss before folks, like my Lady *Fadler* and Sr. *Francis*: Nor goe to *Hide-Park* together the first *Sunday* in a New Chariot, to provoke Eyes and Whispers; And then never to be seen there together again; as if we were proud of one another the first Week, and asham'd of one another for ever After.
>
> (IV. i. 200–6)

Given the examples of contemporary matrimony in Restoration comedy we hardly need a battery of Restoration authorities to justify the extreme caution of Congreve's heroines, Angelica and Millamant. But Halifax's comments on the husbands his own daughter might face definitively substantiate their fears that most Restoration wedding ceremonies were (for upper-class brides) entrances into narrow, if gilded, cages. Halifax frankly warns his daughter that her husband may turn out to be unfaithful, drunken, covetous, ill-humoured, weak, or incompetent, and he gives practical, realistic advice on how to cope with each of these melancholy prospects. For instance, 'when your *Husband* shall resolve to be an *Ass*', you must be very undexterous if you 'do not take care he may be *your Ass* . . . do like a wise *Minister* to an easie *Prince*; first give him the Orders you afterwards receive from him' (pp. 59–60). In any event, his daughter should not expect happiness from marriage, and Halifax fills his advice on marriage with poignant warnings: 'You are therefore to make the best of what is *setled* . . . by *Law*, and not vainly imagine, that it will be *changed* for your sake' (p. 32). 'I will conclude this Article with my Advice, that you would, as much as Nature will give you leave, endeavour to forget the great *Indulgence* you have found at home. After such a gentle Discipline as you have been under; every thing you dislike will seem the harsher to you' (pp. 66–7). And before she recovers her cool poise, Millamant herself reaches something of the same conclusion, 'If Mirabell should not prove a good husband, I am a lost thing.'

Of course we know that Mirabell will be a good husband, but it is nevertheless not surprising that Millamant's confession of love comes only after reflection, and is accompanied by fear. And Millamant has, in fact, been afraid all along. Throughout the comedy she constantly breaks off her sentences, a stylistic device which contemporary playwrights used to reveal 'some affection, as either of sorrow, bashfulness, fear, anger or vehemency':[13] 'Well, I won't have you *Mirabell*—I'm resolv'd—I think—You may go—Ha, ha, ha' (II. i. 456–8); 'Well then—I'll take my death I'm in a horrid fright—*Fainall*, I shall never say it—well—I think —I'll endure you' (IV. i. 288–90). This nervous style is characteristic of Millamant throughout the play, and the nervousness behind all her bravura and arrogance seems fully justified. Except in the

[13] John Smith's definition of *aposiopesis* in *The Mysterie of Rhetorique Unveil'd* (1673), p. 142. See also *Sir Martin Mar-all* in *The Works of John Dryden*, ix, ed. John Loftis and Vinton A. Dearing (Berkeley, Cal., 1966), I. i. 94–6:

> *Lady Dupe.* [I will] seem to strive to put my passion off, yet shew it still by small mistakes.
> *Mrs. Christian.* And broken Sentences.

scenes with Mirabell, whom she is not quite ready to trust, she is surrounded by impossible relatives (her fortune and future are in the hands of Lady Wishfort) and a protective convoy of fools. Nevertheless, Congreve's young heroine handles her difficult economic, personal, and social situations without ever losing humour, poise, self-control, or charm.

Millamant's plight reflects Congreve's dramatic concern with the problems of experiencing genuine emotion and still behaving with due decorum within a world of artificiality. *The Way of the World* thus brings us full circle from *The Man of Mode*, which was concerned with various methods of suppressing emotion in order to behave with brilliant artificiality. Still, neither Millamant nor Mirabell throws good sense or good manners to the winds for the sake of sheer, unmitigated passion. Mirabell sees to it that the financial situation is well in hand, and Millamant sees to it that she can maintain as much autonomy and glamour as possible even after marriage. This measure of control, this degree of calculation, seems inevitably necessary in any world where some degree of artifice and a large degree of economic and social realism are necessary in order to survive (but where the expression of emotion beyond artifice is equally necessary in order to live richly and fully instead of merely managing to exist by duly observing the proper forms). Congreve's hero and heroine are thus experts in the art of social survival; they both manage to control the society around them. For instance, Mirabell was a 'cautious friend' to Mrs. Fainall in more ways than one when, by protecting her financially from Fainall, he also protected himself. But equally clearly, the marriage provisos between Mirabell and Millamant represent the ways of wedlock of the truewits of this world, who can manage to have content as well as form, a good marriage as well as the reputation for one. Nevertheless (and alternatively) the play suggests that it is perfectly possible for a Fainall to 'bustle through' the same world by going through the forms of marriage without feeling any true intimacy, and by having love affairs without feeling any love. It is also (and alternatively) possible that if they can face up to the social and economic facts of their marital situation, the Fainalls themselves may be able to find some means 'well-managed' to 'live easily together'. *The Way of the World* thus always remains clearly and exclusively comic. Neither Congreve, Mirabell, Millamant, nor, for that matter, Halifax, considers their world intolerable. Though they have no illusions about it, they all agree that people can—people must—make the best of it, without self-pity or even loss of humour. Like its hero and heroine, the play in which they appear does not reject its dramatic and social truths. It accepts them. The whole play is affirmative. And ultimately, it exhibits for our own delight (and by way of it, our speculation) a world which is no better, but certainly no worse, than our own. For if Congreve's world contains a full quota of fools and knaves to be got round, it also contains (in the words of Tom Jones describing his own world) 'men worthy of the highest friendship and women of the highest love'.

'Love' is the right word. Writing to Congreve in 1695, John Dennis provides us with a good description of this essential feature of *The Way of the World*. Ben Jonson's dialogue, says Dennis, lacks 'that Spirit, that Grace, and that Noble Railery, which are to be found in more Modern Plays, and which are Virtues that ought to be Inseparable from a finish'd Comedy. But there seems to be one thing more wanting than all the rest, and that is Passion, I mean that fine and that delicate Passion, by which the Soul shows its Politeness, ev'n in the midst of its trouble.'[14] Precisely this sort of 'passion' pervades the spirit, grace, and noble raillery of Congreve's greatest comedy. Congreve appears to have been in love with the actress for whom he created Millamant. And maybe something of his own personal passion projects itself within her play. 'I like her with all her faults' can be either the statement of a man in love with a woman, or the statement of an artist in love with his own creation. Shakespeare has his greatest lovers, Antony and Cleopatra, constantly make similar statements about each other, and by doing so he calls attention to his own remarkable characterization of them. For if, in Mirabell's words, 'beauty is the lover's gift' to his lady, it is also the artist's ultimate gift to his work of art. So the unique beauty of *The Way of the*

---

[14] See *William Congreve: Letters and Documents*, ed. John C. Hodges (London, 1964), p. 175.

World may be in part the result of the passion bestowed upon and portrayed within it. And the fact that the passion survives without any illusions is the best possible evidence that it is genuine. There just do not seem to be any illusions at all in *The Way of the World*, and that is why it is never sentimental or false. Clearly the world portrayed (like its heroine) has plenty of faults of its own. It is full of artifice, vanity, conniving, and arrogance, and it poses very real dangers for its inhabitants. But somehow Congreve makes it possible for us both to understand his social world and to like it. He shows us how to accept and enjoy it with all its faults, and ultimately he even allows us to like it for its faults when we relish the lascivious Lady Wishfort and the malicious Fainall, even as we sympathize with Mrs. Fainall and triumph with Mirabell.

There is a very different dramatic world which contains a full quota of knaves and fools, but which also contains men worthy of the highest friendship and women of the highest love, and this is the world of *King Lear*. As in *The Way of the World* there are characters who speak alike and appear alike on first impression, but who later prove to be very different (Albany and Cornwall share the same introductory line). There are characters who only gradually reveal their true natures and their true motives to us and to each other. And we finally distinguish Shakespeare's tragic sheep from his tragic goats, not on the basis of their intelligence or their eloquence, but on the basis of their 'kindness', their true humanity. In fact, *King Lear* may be the most profoundly moral play in the world. It is a play obsessed with moral judgement, and it finally summons its characters to face the ultimate moral judgement. And the ultimate judgement which Shakespeare's characters face is not judgement by their royal peers, nor judgement by the gods, but judgement by common humanity itself, as represented by us, by their audience. But before going any further into the drama's supreme confrontation with the way of our world, it is necessary to give some attention to other kinds of dramatic judgement. A very cursory survey of some other Shakespearian tragedies suggests that there are several different ways of eliciting or discouraging it.

7 'Likenesses of truth': dramatic judgement in some Shakespearian tragedies

L'art est ce qu'il y a de plus réel, la plus austère école de la vie, et le vrai Jugement dernier. PROUST

All my life I have held that you can class people according to how they may be imagined behaving to King Lear. ISAK DINESEN

WRITING about Shakespeare's tragic lovers, some moralistic critics conclude that, for the most part, they get just punishments for their passionate misdeeds. According to this view, for instance, we see Romeo, 'whose nature bears the seeds of its own destruction, bring about the piteous misadventures for which he wrongly blames the stars'.[1] This statement about Romeo raises some interesting questions about the sort of dramatic judgement meted out to him, since it flatly contradicts some of Shakespeare's own statements about the particular kind of dramatic fate which operates so inexorably in *Romeo and Juliet*. It is perfectly true that Romeo blames the stars for his tragic predicament. But, then, so does Shakespeare. Indeed, the very first piece of information that Shakespeare gives us about his Juliet and her Romeo is the fact that they are going to be 'star-crossed' lovers whose sad overthrow finally buries their parents' strife. And with this information firmly planted in our minds by the Prologue, we are supposed to watch 'the fearful passage of their death-mark'd love' which is the two hours' traffic of this specific tragic stage. In *Romeo and Juliet* much of the responsibility for the tragedy lies in the stars, and Shakespeare says so.

[1] Franklin M. Dickey, *Not Wisely but too Well* (San Marino, Cal., 1957), p. 112.

When one remembers the course of action in *Romeo and Juliet* it becomes ever more evident that Shakespeare's young lovers were the pitiable victims of a dramatic destiny which no amount of caution or virtue on their part could have averted. For everything of importance in this play—everything the young lovers do, and everything everyone else does—happens either too early or too late, and thus contributes to the fatal outcome. The deaths of both Romeo and Juliet might have been avoided, for instance, if Friar Lawrence's letter had reached Romeo on time, or if Friar Lawrence had arrived at the tomb a few minutes earlier, or if Juliet had awakened a few minutes earlier, or if Romeo had come to the tomb a few minutes later. And in case anyone might have missed Shakespeare's emphasis on the fatal untimeliness of all these happenings, Friar Lawrence spells everything out for us:

> But when I came, some minute ere the time
> Of her awakening, here untimely lay
> The noble Paris and true Romeo dead.
>
> (v. iii. 256–8)

Obviously, the climax of *Romeo and Juliet* does not stand in isolation from the rest of the play, and in the beginning of the tragedy Shakespeare lays the groundwork for the events to come. To call attention to the consequences of untimely events, Shakespeare establishes verbal connections between inopportune happenings and disaster at least three times in the first act. Three characters, with different personalities, in different contexts, discuss events that may take place too early or too late, and worry that such untimeliness may have dire consequences. Old Capulet tells Paris that Juliet is too young for marriage (Shakespeare himself altered his source in order to make his heroine extremely young). When Paris answers that women even younger than Juliet are mothers, Capulet says, 'And too soon marr'd are those so early made' (i. ii. 13). Amidst this light banter is the suggestion that events which happen too soon will cause harm. Capulet then says of Juliet, the 'Earth hath swallowed all my hopes but she' (i. ii. 14). In these lines, Shakespeare quickly establishes casual connections between early weddings, potential disaster, and graves. Of course anyone might easily miss, forget, or ignore these lines, so Shakespeare repeats himself. On the way to Capulet's party, Benvolio tells Romeo, 'Supper is done, and we shall come too late', and Romeo answers,

> I fear, too early; for my mind misgives
> Some consequence, yet hanging in the stars,
> Shall bitterly begin his fearful date
> With this night's revels . . .
>
> (I. iv. 105–9)

Romeo's foreboding echoes, with increased intensity, Capulet's association of untimely events and disaster, and Romeo adds a connection between such events and consequences hanging in the stars. Then Shakespeare makes the same points with even greater clarity when he gives the collocation of ideas to Juliet. Acknowledging her love for Romeo and her fears for the future, Juliet says, 'If he be married, / My grave is like to be my wedding bed' (I. v. 132–3). The Nurse tells Juliet that Romeo is a Montague, and Juliet exclaims,

> My only love sprung from my only hate!
> Too early seen unknown, and known too late!
> Prodigious birth of love it is to me,
> That I must love a loathed enemy.
>
> (I. v. 136–9)

Yet again, Shakespeare brings together references to graves, weddings, untimely events, and deadly consequences. And Juliet's foreboding includes her sense of complete helplessness in the face of fatally inopportune timing. Had she known earlier that Romeo was a Montague, she might not have loved him. But the information that he was her family's enemy came after she had fallen irrevocably in love. Where Romeo feared some consequences hanging in the stars, Juliet tells us that the consequences have begun.

Why does Shakespeare repeat his 'too early, too late' theme in such different contexts? Why not give the set of ideas to a single character? Certainly Shakespeare gives the speeches increasing seriousness as the mood of the play darkens, coming as they do

from a befuddled old Capulet, then from a vaguely worried
Romeo, and finally from an impassioned Juliet. But Shakespeare
may have distributed the same set of ideas to various characters
in order to indicate that the connection between untimely events
and tragic consequences is a general state of affairs, a pervading
atmosphere, a fact of life and death in the world of this particular
play,[2] and that the recognition of this fact is not an insight limited
to any single person. In any case, by the end of the first act, Shakespeare's repetition of these ideas has directed his audience to
expect tragic consequences from any events that come too early
or too late, and along with dramatic expectation goes a dramatic
appetite, an aesthetic desire to see these expectations fulfilled.

Later, in order to avoid the marriage to Paris, Juliet agrees to
drink the friar's potion in spite of her terror that she might wake
up 'before the time' that Romeo comes to rescue her (IV. iii.
30–2). So the preparations for Juliet's untimely wedding become
preparations for her more untimely funeral. As characters lament,
lines from the first act are echoed and proved to be prophetic.
Juliet's grave is like to be her marriage-bed. Too soon marred is
she so early made. Capulet's lines, 'my child is dead, / And with
my child my joys are buried' (IV. v. 63–4) echoes his earlier line,
'The earth hath swallowed all my hopes but she'. Thus, in the
fourth act of *Romeo and Juliet*, the audience watches the past of the
play invade the present, and of course the pseudo-catastrophe
ironically foreshadows the final catastrophe.

In the end of this play, everything that we have expected to
happen does happen, though not necessarily in the way we
expected it to happen. The false death of Juliet becomes the real
death of Juliet. She had dreaded waking up too early; she does
wake up too late to save Romeo. Juliet toasts Romeo with the
Friar's potion in the fourth act; Romeo toasts Juliet with real
poison in the fifth. So where, from the beginning of the play,
Shakespeare led us to expect ultimate disaster from a series of
untimely events, he dramatically satisfies our expectation in the
end. And his network of untimely events most certainly influences

---

[2] Contrast the comic consequences of the series of untimely events in *The Comedy of Errors*.

our final view of the characters. Impulsive actions and cautious plans alike contribute to the tragic results. The actions of old characters (like Capulet) as well as the actions of Shakespeare's ardent young lovers all come at the wrong time, and all contribute to the play's outcome. Time after time, the best-laid plans of Friar Lawrence go just as awry as the spontaneous actions of the young people. And the very best motives (those of the Friar) are no more a hedge against dramatic destiny than the worst motives (those of Tybalt). Shakespeare thus takes any responsibility for their sad fate away from his hero and heroine, since his series of seemingly arbitrary coincidences makes it obvious that character is not destiny in *Romeo and Juliet*. The same Juliet might have awakened earlier. The same Friar might have delivered the message (to the same Romeo) on time if the plague had not intervened. The coincidences in the play indicate that no amount of caution or haste on the part of the characters could have averted the tragedy. Thus we are left to pity the young couple and to blame feuds, fate, or coincidence—never the young lovers—for the sad ending. At the same time, the inexorable nature of the pattern that traps Romeo and Juliet gives us the aesthetic satisfaction of seeing a dramatic design work itself out. We can pity the characters and we can also experience satisfaction while watching Shakespeare's tragic stars in operation. *Romeo and Juliet*, then (and again), is not the story of any crime and punishment on the part of its hero and heroine. It is the dramatic representation of the 'misadventur'd piteous overthrows' described in its Prologue.

Would it be better otherwise? Would we prefer a cautionary sermon? Surely there is far more validity inherent in the play as it stands. For there are many things in everyday life which can go wrong because of their timing. There are 'misadventur'd piteous overthrows' that nothing we do can prevent or remedy. *Romeo and Juliet* is about such things. In retrospect, we can see that the inherent condition of life in Shakespeare's Verona made everything go wrong. Finally (and too late) the Capulets and Montagues bury the feud that killed Romeo and Juliet along with the bodies of the children who died too early. But their children had nothing to do with the original feud, nothing to do with the *donnée* of the play, nothing to do with the condition of conflict, danger, and hatred in the world that (like a contagious plague) may take down innocent and guilty people alike. It is comforting to imagine a world where virtue would have been rewarded, and death would have been averted, if only Romeo had behaved himself properly. But this is the ideal world of moralistic criticism, and not the infinitely sadder, but infinitely more realistic, world of *Romeo and Juliet*.

In other tragedies Shakespeare gives his characters greater responsibility for their own destinies. 'The fault' in *Julius Caesar* 'is not in the stars', but in the characters themselves; and the construction of this political tragedy differs sharply from the organization of *Romeo and Juliet*. Shakespeare could not assume that his audience knew the story of Romeo and Juliet, and therefore he had to create his own kind of fixed fate, his own pattern of tragic inevitability. In *Julius Caesar*, Shakespeare can take our foreknowledge of the outcome for granted. Dramatic inevitability is built into his historical subject. And so, from the very beginning of *Julius Caesar*, Shakespeare sets his complex presentation of the characters and events against the back-drop of our absolute certainty concerning the outcome of the action.

In *Julius Caesar*, Shakespeare deals with historical characters and situations that were topics of controversy in his time. The controversy lay between those who abhorred the murder of Caesar and those who applauded the elimination of a tyrant.[3] In Sir Thomas Elyot's *Boke Named The Governour*, which was one of the sources for Shakespeare's play, both these attitudes are held in solution. Elyot's discussion of Caesar (like Shakespeare's presentation of him) mingles high praise and blame:

Julius Cesar, who, beinge nat able to sustaine the burden of fortune, and enuienge his owne felicitie, abandoned his naturall disposition, and as it were, beinge dronke with ouer moche welth, sought newe

---

[3] See D. A. Traversi, *Shakespeare: The Roman Plays* (Stanford, Cal., 1963), p. 11; Terence Spencer, 'Shakespeare and the Elizabethan Romans', *Shakespeare Survey*, x (1957), 27–38; and Geoffrey Bullough, *Narrative and Dramatic Sources of Shakespeare* (London, 1964), pp. 17–29.

wayes howe to be aduaunced aboue the astate of mortall princes. Wherfore litle and litle he withdrewe from men his accustomed gentilnesse, becomyng more sturdy in langage, and straunge in countenance, than euer before had ben his usage. . . . wherby he so dyd alienate from hym the hartis of his most wise and assured adherentis, that, from that tyme forwarde, his life was to them tedious, and abhorring him as a monstre or commune enemie, they beinge knitte in a confederacy slewe hym sitting in the Senate; of whiche conspiraci was chiefe capitaine, Marcus Brutus, whome of all other he beste loued, for his great wisedome and prowesse. . . . Thus Cesar, by omittinge his olde affabilitie, dyd incende his next frendes and companions to sle hym. . . . Who beholdinge the cause of the dethe of this moste noble Cesar, unto whom in eloquence, doctrine, martiall prowesse, and gentilnesse, no prince may be comparid, and the acceleration or haste to his confusion, causid by his owne edict or decre, will nat commende affabilitie and extolle libertie of speche?[4]

According to Elyot, then, Caesar had become proud and arbitrary, and thus he contributed to his own destruction. Nevertheless (and at the same time) Caesar was still incomparable. He was 'the moste noble Cesar', a very great man. A similar mixture of blame and praise appears in Elyot's discussion of Brutus and Cassius. For Elyot, the two conspirators were noble Romans who acted out of worthy intentions, but who misconstrued the nature and result of their actions, and rightly suffered the consequences:

Brutus and Cassius, two noble Romaynes, and men of excellent vertues, whiche, pretendinge an honorable zeale to the libertie and commune weale of their citie, slewe Julius Cesar (who trusted them moste of all other) for that he usurped to haue the perpetuall dominion of the empire, supposinge thereby to haue brought the senate and people to their pristinate libertie. But it dyd nat so succede to their purpose. But by the dethe of so noble a prince hapned confusion and ciuile batayles. And bothe Brutus and Cassius, after longe warres vainquisshed by Octauian, neuewe and hiere unto Cesar, at the last

---

[4] *The Boke, Named the Governour*, ed. Henry Croft (London, 1880), vol. ii, pp. 47–51. For Shakespeare's use of Elyot in *Julius Caesar* see J. C. Maxwell, '*Julius Caesar* and Elyot's *Governour*', N & Q, n.s. iii (1956), 147, and Bullough, *Narrative and Dramatic Sources of Shakespeare*, pp. 22–3, 166–8 (where the relevant passages are quoted in full).

falling in to extreme desperation, slewe them selfes. A worthy and conuenient vengeaunce for the murder of so noble and valyaunt a prince.[5]

Shakespeare's play reflects (and requires) a similar ambivalence towards the major characters and events. Time after time, scenes which present the individual characters in an unfavourable light are balanced by scenes which present them very favourably, so that the audience itself is encouraged alternately to blame and praise the various characters. In *Julius Caesar* a series of fatal misconstructions made by the characters themselves creates the tragic pattern, while Shakespeare's audience watches the characters misconstrue the nature and consequences of their own actions with the retrospective foreknowledge of a historian, a playwright, or a god, who can know what no mortal, trapped in the course of history itself, can ever know; that is, he can know with absolute certainty exactly what will happen next.[6] In everyday life (like Caesar, Brutus, and Cassius) we cannot know for sure what the results of our actions and decisions may be. As members of the audience watching *Julius Caesar*, we possess privileged information about the consequences of the actions taken by Brutus, Cassius, and Caesar from the very moment we enter the theatre. This privileged information gives dramatic irony to almost every decision made within the play. And from the outset, by means of several expository scenes, Shakespeare makes it clear that misconstructions on the part of the various characters will shape the action of *Julius Caesar*. When Casca and Cicero discuss the significance of the great storm, Cicero concludes,

> Indeed, it is a strange-disposed time;
> But men may construe things after their fashion,
> Clean from the purpose of the things themselves.
>
> (I. iii. 33–5)

---

[5] *The Governour*, vol. ii, pp. 244–5.

[6] See J. H. Hexter, *Reappraisals in History* (London, 1967), pp. 10–11: 'The saddest words of tongue or pen may be, "It might have been." The most human are, "If only I had known." But it is precisely characteristic of the historian that he does know. He is really sure what is going to happen next, not in his time as a pilgrim here below, but in his own time as a historian. . . . It might be better to say that while men are ordinarily trying to connect the present with a future that is to be, the historian connects his present with a future that has already been.'

Throughout *Julius Caesar* men bring tragedy upon themselves, upon others, and upon the state, because they construe things after their own fashion, clean from the purpose of the things themselves. Various characters misconstrue the significance of the storm and of their various dreams. Characters mistake friends and foes: Caesar trusts Brutus, Brutus trusts Antony. The conspirators tragically misconstrue the results of the deed they plan. Caesar, Cassius, and Brutus all misinterpret their own abilities as well as the motives of others. Such misconstructions and the destruction that results from them form a major pattern in *Julius Caesar*. Made up of the stuff of history, this play shows us the tragic vulnerability of the individuals who themselves make history. They see what they believe to be true. They then take actions which they hope and believe will bring good consequences for themselves or for their nation. But the literal consequences of their actions may differ from, they may in fact be the opposite of, the consequences which the given individuals imagined and ex-pected. And thus the makers of history have to take the responsi-bility for historical consequences which they themselves did not anticipate.

The series of parallel death scenes in this play illustrates Shake-speare's dramatic concern with fatal misconstructions. When Shakespeare shows us the murder of Cinna the poet, he establishes some parallels between the death of this minor figure and the death of Caesar himself. In the great assassination scene, Caesar was surrounded by people who he believed were his friends, and then he was stabbed by them. Brutus, who bore no personal grudge against Caesar ('I know no personal cause to spurn at him, / But for the general' (II. i. 11–12)), stabbed Caesar in order to restore liberty by ridding Rome of Caesar's spirit, of Caesarism, of the tyranny that the name of Caesar seemed to imply. The first person to follow Caesar is Cinna the poet. Cinna introduces him-self to us with the statement, 'I dreamt to-night that I did feast with Caesar' (III. iii. 1). Then, when Cinna gives the plebeians his name, they confuse him with Cinna the conspirator, and thus they construe things after their own fashion. The terrified poet tells them he is not the conspirator, but the plebeians reply that it does not matter, for his name has already doomed him. What's in a name in *Julius Caesar*? Cassius earlier asked the question about Caesar himself (I. ii. 142-9). The plebeians have no personal grudge against Cinna the poet any more than Brutus had a personal grudge against Caesar, and their unthinking violence is an example of the violence that is released as a consequence of Caesar's murder.

We cannot say that Brutus was no better than a member of the mob that senselessly murdered Cinna. Indeed, Brutus' noble motives clearly contrast with the heedless violence of the plebeians. Nevertheless, the horror of the Cinna scene makes the group murder (for whatever reason) of any individual who is unable to defend himself seem terribly wrong. Certainly both scenes dramatically emphasize the complete helplessness of the individual against those who would destroy him for 'no personal cause', but for some abstract, arbitrary reason. Furthermore, the death of Cinna involves Antony in the horrors that result from the death of Caesar. By assassinating Caesar, Brutus and the conspirators trigger retaliation from Antony; and by his inflammatory speech to the populace, Antony looses the forces that destroy Cinna. Now both the assassination and the inflammatory speech were perfectly justifiable from the individual points of view of Brutus and of Antony, though from a historical point of view both actions bring about tragic, disastrous consequences. Thus, in spite of the fact that no one in this play is without some just cause for his actions, no one in the play is without responsibility for the suffering caused by his actions.

The next person to die on the stage is Cassius, whose death involves yet another set of fatal misconstructions. In the fifth act, Cassius sends Titinius to find out whether the troops in the distance are friends or foes. Pindarus reports to Cassius that Titinius has been surrounded by horsemen, who shout for joy. Misinterpreting the evidence, Pindarus and Cassius conclude that Titinius was taken by the enemy, and Cassius commits suicide. Titinius returns, and finding the body of Cassius, he asks:

> Why didst thou send me forth, brave Cassius?
> Did I not meet thy friends, and did not they

Put on my brows this wreath of victory,
And bid me give it thee? Didst thou not hear their shouts?
Alas, thou hast misconstrued every thing!

(v. iii. 80–4)

Once again, misconstruction causes disaster. The evidence was perceived accurately but its meaning was misinterpreted. Interestingly, Cassius' 'weak eyesight' made it impossible for him to distinguish between friends and foes, and a list of characters who mistake friends and foes in *Julius Caesar* would include practically every major character in the play. According to Virgil K. Whitaker, the most serious weakness of *Julius Caesar* 'from the point of view of moral exposition is undoubtedly Brutus' own failure to recognize the enormity of his mistake'.[7] But Brutus' failure is part of the larger action. It is part of the tragic meaning of this play. It is typical of the tendency, exhibited by everyone in the tragedy, to interpret their own weaknesses as strengths and to interpret their own delusions as certainties.[8] 'Alas, thou hast misconstrued everything,' says Titinius to the dead Cassius. The same statement provides us with a perfect comment on Brutus as well. It also provides us with a perfect comment on the tragic limits of human perception. And the misconstructions that these limits inevitably cause is what this historical tragedy is all about. For the personal perspectives of historical beings—however objective they try to be—are bound to be influenced by individual ambitions, hopes, and ideals. As fallible mortals, the characters inevitably see what they dream or imagine or believe to be true, and then they interpret their personal visions of truth as if they were empirical reality. Or rather, they superimpose their dreams of truth upon the facts before them. Sometimes empirical reality and the truths of the imagination are one and the same, but in this tragedy they are not. Time after time, what the various characters sincerely believe is true turns out not to be true at all.

Even as the characters in *Julius Caesar* constantly misinterpret the evidence before them, Shakespeare's pattern of tragic misconstruction extends to include the audience itself. Shakespeare

[7] See Whitaker's *The Mirror up to Nature* (San Marino, Cal., 1965), p. 132.
[8] Traversi, *Shakespeare: The Roman Plays*, p. 31.

shows the members of his audience that they, too, easily may misconstrue things. For instance, Antony's speech to the Roman mob influences the sympathies of Shakespeare's audience as well. 'We, as an audience,' says Granville-Barker, 'are apt to join our-selves to the audience in the Forum without further question', and it is, indeed, Antony's duty to see that we do so.[9] In the end, if we are inclined to judge Brutus too severely, Brutus dies grandly, and Antony's speech rehabilitates him. Similarly, if we are inclined to look down on Antony, his fair and warm speech in final praise of Brutus causes admiration for Antony himself. Any absolute black or white moral judgement is prohibited.

In his study of *Julius Caesar*, Adrien Bonjour concludes that 'It looks indeed as if Shakespeare wanted "to prove the moral value of suspended judgment." And before it is suspended, our judg-ment has been constantly questioned, shifted and revised: in fact, Shakespeare made of *Julius Caesar* the drama of divided sympa-thies.'[10] Certainly there is no idealized hero in this play, and there is no absolute villain. In the last analysis, Dr. Johnson's famous statement provides the best of all glosses on the characters in *Julius Caesar*:

> Shakespeare has no heroes; his scenes are occupied only by men . . . Dennis and Rymer think his Romans not sufficiently Roman, and Voltaire censures his kings as not completely royal. . . . But Shakespeare always makes nature predominate over accident; and, if he preserves the essential character, is not very careful of distinctions superinduced and adventitious. His story requires Romans or Kings, but he thinks only on men.

The characters in *Julius Caesar* are always portrayed as fallible men, and Shakespeare implies that the audience at his own play is rather like the 'tag–rag' group of plebeians who clap Caesar and hiss him 'according as he pleas'd and displeas'd them, as they use to do the players in the theatre' (I. ii. 256–60). And so we clap and hiss

---

[9] Harley Granville-Barker, *Preface to the Tragedie of Julius Caesar* (London, 1926), p. xl. For a fascinating discussion of Antony's manipulation of audience responses see Kenneth Burke, 'Antony in Behalf of the Play', in *Perspectives by Incongruity*, ed. Stanley Edgar Hyman (Bloomington, Ind., 1964), pp. 64–75.

[10] Adrien Bonjour, *The Structure of Julius Caesar* (Liverpool, 1958), p. 3.

Shakespeare's Romans, according as they please or displease us. Shakespeare thus manipulates the sympathies and the perceptions of the audience at a tragedy which is (partly at least) about perception. In this tragedy of human error, we both pity and blame the characters while we watch their misconstructions create the tragic design. For the fault in *Julius Caesar* lies in human nature itself, since human nature makes it inevitable that mortal men will construe things after their fashion, clean from the purpose of the things themselves. And who, in the play or in its audience, is so firm that he may not be seduced by his own misconstructions? (I. ii. 311.)

In *Romeo and Juliet* characters (with the exception of Tybalt) tend to be well-meaning, and in *Julius Caesar* characters usually feel that there is some just cause for their deeds. Caesar, in fact, was ambitious, and Brutus was an honourable man. Shakespeare adopts a very different dramatic point of view towards Macbeth, who, placed in the same sort of situation as Brutus, deliberately dares do more than may become a man. The structural similarities between *Julius Caesar* and *Macbeth* are obvious. Like Brutus, Macbeth decides to kill a ruler who trusts him, does so, and suffers the consequences of his deed. But in *Macbeth* we find a terrible exaggeration of the situation. Macbeth's motives are never noble or honourable, and Duncan is far more idealized than Caesar. While Brutus misconstrues the significance and probable consequences of his deed, Macbeth has full knowledge of the implications of his decision and of its certain consequences before he actually murders Duncan. If the action of *Julius Caesar* stresses human error, the action of Macbeth emphasizes the nature of mortal sin.[11] Distinctions between good and evil, right and wrong, are far clearer in *Macbeth*, where the forces of heaven and hell extend the ramifications of Macbeth's tragedy to cosmic proportions.

In *Macbeth* Shakespeare's use of the supernatural is significantly extended. In *Romeo and Juliet*, which is the personal and domestic

[11] For full discussion of *Macbeth* as a tragedy of 'judgment here' see Dame Helen Gardner, 'Milton's "Satan" and the Theme of Damnation in Elizabethan Tragedy', *Essays and Studies* (1948), pp. 46–66.

tragedy of young lovers and their families, there are dreams that come true, dreams that are highly personal to the dreamer. In *Julius Caesar*, Brutus and Calpurnia dream private dreams, but the storm is public, manifesting itself to all Rome, since the fall of Caesar involves the fate of an empire as well as the fate of families and individuals. And of course Caesar's ghost rises to tell Brutus that he cannot escape the consequences of his actions. In *Macbeth* we find all the supernatural elements from these earlier plays, and more. In *Macbeth* there are dreams, storms, ghosts, and (above all) there are witches. The very first scene of this tragedy is in fact an expository scene which supplies a frame of reference for the subsequent action, since the over-all movement of *Macbeth* is unified by mysterious patterns of equivocation. Everything the witches say is equivocal; the Porter gives an extended discussion of the nature of equivocation; Macbeth, Lady Macbeth, Malcolm, Macbeth's servants and soldiers, all either deliberately equivocate or they are forced to do so. And only finally, to his tragic horror, does Macbeth doubt the 'equivocation of the fiend / That lies like truth' (v. v. 44).

The witches begin the chain of equivocation. They supply the audience, and then Macbeth, with equivocal foreknowledge of the future. From one point of view, they represent fate, and Macbeth, interpreting their statements wrongly, of his own free will fulfils their prophecies in ways he could not have foreseen. In a discussion of *Macbeth*, Frank Kermode gives detailed attention to the initial equivocations of the witches:

> 1 *Witch.* When shall we three meet again?
>   In thunder, lightning, or in rain?
> 2 *Witch.* When the hurlyburly's done,
>   When the battle's lost and won.

As Kermode points out, hurlies are to burlies as thunder is to lightning (you can hardly have one without the other), and 'lost battles are normally also won'. The witches' statements (Kermode says) are parodies of prophetic equivocation, and *Macbeth* is above all a play of prophecy: 'it not only enacts prophecies, it is obsessed by them. . . . It is about failures to attend to the part of equivoque which lacks immediate interest (as if one should attend to hurly and not to burly).'[12] Even the sex of the witches is equivocal; Banquo cannot decide whether they are men or women:

> You should be women,
> And yet your beards forbid me to interpret
> That you are so.
>
> (I. iii. 45–7)

The witches can be taken either way. They are women, and they are not women. Ambiguity of sex later becomes a tragic sign of equivocation in the play. Lady Macbeth asks the spirits that tend on mortal thoughts to unsex her, and in doing so she reminds us of the witches. Macbeth worries about his manhood throughout the play, and daring to do more than does become a man, he becomes no man, and Shakespeare metaphorically associates him with beasts and devils.

Because equivocation is so important in this play, it is useful to mention a contemporary definition of the term that is now obsolete: 'Equivocal. Equal. Or the same in name (with something else) but not in reality—having a name without the qualities it implies.' In *Macbeth*, characters have the name of woman without womanly qualities; they have the name of men without the qualities that distinguish men from beasts; they have the name of King without genuinely kingly qualities. The illustration that the *Oxford English Dictionary* gives of this definition is from Ussher's *Power of Princes* (1661): 'They . . . were but equivocal Kings, such in name, but not in deed.' Macbeth finally holds the name of King, but he never feels that he really is King of Scotland; while Duncan, the rightful King, was described as 'clear' (the opposite of equivocal) by Macbeth himself:

> this Duncan
> Hath borne his faculties so meek, hath been
> So clear in his great office . . .
>
> (I. vii. 16–18)

[12] Frank Kermode, *The Sense of an Ending* (New York, 1967), pp. 83–4. For further discussion of equivocation in *Macbeth* see Kenneth Muir's Introduction to the Arden *Macbeth* (London, 1951).

In contrast, Macbeth himself always feels like a mere player-king, who is costumed in strange and inappropriate garments that do not fit. For in order first to gain the crown and then to keep it, Macbeth and Lady Macbeth must continually equivocate, play-act, and put on shows:

> Away, and mock the time with fairest show;
> False face must hide what the false heart doth know.
>
> (I. vii. 81–2)

> . . . make our faces vizards to our hearts,
> Disguising what they are.
>
> (III. ii. 34–5)

When the witches equivocate, their prophecies lead Macbeth and his wife to equivocate and to infect their whole world with equivocations. In the words of the play, 'nothing is but what is not' (I. iii. 141). Macbeth calls Banquo's ghost an unreal mockery, a horrible shadow (III. iv. 106); but the reality that Banquo's ghost represents is genuine, and the kingly part Macbeth tries to play at the banquet is itself an unreal mockery. Macbeth's feast is always Banquo's banquet. Macbeth is and is not really King of Scotland. The ghost is and is not real. Later, the witches stage a deliberately equivocal show for Macbeth:

> 1 *Witch.*   Show!
> 2 *Witch.*   Show!
> 3 *Witch.*   Show!
> *All.*   Show his eyes, and grieve his heart;
> Come like shadows, so depart!
>
> (IV. i. 107–11)

And their show ultimately operates on Macbeth in exactly the way that the Porter's equivocating liquor operates on lechery: 'it makes him, and it mars him; it sets him on, and it takes him off; it persuades him, and disheartens him; makes him stand to, and not stand to; in conclusion, equivocates him . . . and, giving him the lie, leaves him' (II. iii. 27–34).

After the murder of Duncan, fair seems foul, and foul seems fair. The innocent sons of Duncan seem guilty, and the guilty

Macbeth acts innocent. Everything can be interpreted in two ways. Even the idealized Malcolm is forced to play-act to Macduff; the fair prince has to describe himself as foul, since

> That which you are, my thoughts cannot transpose;
> Angels are bright still, though the brightest fell.
> Though all things foul would wear the brows of grace,
> Yet grace must still look so.
>
> (IV. iii. 21–4)

Along with Malcolm, Macbeth's servants must equivocate. Macbeth has only mouth-honour, not the thing itself. He is served by constrained things, 'Whose hearts are absent too' (V. iv. 14). Finally, Macbeth sees Birnam Forest come to Dunsinane, and he recognizes the diabolical nature of equivocations that 'palter with us in a double sense', that separate the literal truth from the emotional truth, that separate the symbol from the thing symbolized, that keep the word of promise to our ear, and break it to our hope (V. viii. 20–2).

All the references to equivocation, to acting, to disguising the self, underline the most potent psychological reality exhibited in *Macbeth*: by being false to the King, Macbeth is false to himself. Ironically, Macbeth is damned not because he had the courage to be evil, but because he lacked the courage to remain true to the better side of his own equivocal nature. As Macbeth knows perfectly well at the beginning (I. vii. 11–28), his true manhood, his true identity, depend upon his remaining a loyal subject, a loyal general, a loyal kinsman to the King, an honourable man with the 'milk of human kindness'[13] in his veins:

> I dare do all that may become a man;
> Who dares do more is none.
>
> (I. vii. 46–7)

> We will proceed no further in this business.
> He hath honour'd me of late; and I have bought
> Golden opinions from all sorts of people . . .
>
> (I. vii. 31–3)

[13] 'Kindness', in *Macbeth* and *King Lear* means 'type'—'the milk of human-kind, of human nature'—as well as kindly behaviour. To be 'unkind' in both plays is to be unnatural, to be inhuman.

But Lady Macbeth denies Macbeth's clear recognition of the truth about himself. She claims that, because she herself would not hesitate to kill the King for personal advantage, she is therefore the better 'man' of the two. And at some point during her tirade insulting his manhood, Macbeth weakens and asks only, 'If we should fail?' Then, after hearing Lady Macbeth's arguments that they cannot fail, Macbeth accepts his wife's definition of manhood ('Bring forth men-children only'). He decides to start acting, to start physically and emotionally becoming false to himself, as well as to the King:

> I am settled, and bend up
> Each corporal agent to this terrible feat.
> Away, and mock the time with fairest show;
> False face must hide what the false heart doth know.
> (I. vii. 79–82)

Henceforth, from one point of view, Macbeth can never be more than a poor player. And henceforth, from another point of view, Macbeth cannot keep from mutating into an inhuman monster. Both of these points of view, at one time or another in the play, are Macbeth's own. For in contrast to Richard III, who fulfils his own dramatically established, unequivocally evil nature by resolving to prove himself a great villain, Macbeth violates his own originally good nature by doing so. Given the point of view of modern psychology, *Macbeth* may be seen as a tragedy of the 'forfeited self', a tragedy that shows us exactly what happens when an individual violates his own 'intrinsic conscience':

This [intrinsic conscience] is based upon the unconscious and pre-conscious perception of our own nature, of our own destiny, or our own capacities, of our own 'call' in life.

It insists that we be true to our inner nature and that we do not deny it out of weakness or for advantage or for any other reason. He who belies his talent, the born painter who sells stockings instead, the intelligent man who lives a stupid life, the man who sees the truth and keeps his mouth shut, the coward who gives up his manliness, all these people perceive in a deep way that they have done wrong to themselves and despise themselves for it.[14]

[14] A. H. Maslow, *Toward a Psychology of Being* (Princeton, N.J., 1962), p. 6.

From the moment that he considers murdering Duncan, Macbeth experiences (in his own words) 'judgment here'. Though he escapes punishment from the other characters until the very end, Macbeth's own forfeited self sits in judgement upon him from the moment that he forfeits it. And at the black summit of his life, Macbeth can define what he has become only in terms of what he can no longer be. He can only compare himself, negatively, to the man that he once was, to the man that he might have been:

> I have liv'd long enough. My way of life
> Is fall'n into the sear, the yellow leaf;
> And that which should accompany old age,
> As honour, love, obedience, troops of friends,
> I must not look to have; but, in their stead,
> Curses not loud but deep, mouth-honour, breath,
> Which the poor heart would fain deny, and dare not.
>
> (v. iii. 22–8)

At the end of the play Macbeth has, and he knows that he has, precisely nothing. And his loss of everything that he once was, and therefore of everything that he once had, is Macbeth's real punishment. Certainly Macbeth himself had long ago realized that he had already lived quite 'long enough':

> Had I but died an hour before this chance,
> I had liv'd a blessed time; for, from this instant,
> There's nothing serious in mortality—
> All is but toys.
>
> (ii. iii. 89–92)

Throughout the action of his tragedy, Macbeth suffers incomparably more than any of his victims. 'After life's fitful fever', Duncan 'sleeps well', while after the murder of Duncan, Macbeth sleeps not at all. Macbeth's death comes as no particular punishment to him. If anything, it appears to come as a kind of release from a life that, so far as everyone on the stage is concerned, signifies nothing.

Thus, whether or not the gods summon Macbeth to any judgement in the after-life, and long before he faces retributive judgement from his peers, Macbeth always and still faces his own total self-condemnation. And maybe we all, in the last analysis, finally must judge ourselves, as Macbeth judges himself, on the basis of our truth to our personal integrity. From this psychological point of view, and its analogous dramatic point of view, it is easy to understand why, in clear contrast to Macbeth, characters like Hamlet, Cleopatra, and Brutus can die quite content with themselves and with their dramatic destinies. For within their tragedies, these characters do whatever being true to their dramatically determined integrity requires them to do. They each thus can say that they 'parted well' and paid their score:

> *Brutus.*   Thy life hath had some smatch of honour in it. . . .
> Farewell, good Strato. Caesar, now be still.
> I kill'd not thee with half so good a will.

> *Cleopatra.*   Husband, I come.
> Now to that name my courage prove my title!
> I am fire and air; my other elements
> I give to baser life.

> *Hamlet.*   Horatio, I am dead:
> Thou livest; report me and my cause aright
> To the unsatisfied.

All these characters go down (in the words which Eliot applied to Hamlet) 'fairly well pleased' with themselves. For they each accept and fulfil the destinies inherent in the nature given them by their creator. Thus we do not feel for them the same kind of bitter grief that we feel for Macbeth who wilfully, deliberately, and with malice aforethought forfeited his manhood, his humanity, and his integrity and therefore concludes that, at best, he can only go down fighting like a brute beast:

> I gin to be aweary of the sun,
> And wish th'estate o'th'world were now undone.
> Ring the alarum bell. Blow wind, come wrack;
> At least we'll die with harness on our back.
>   (v. v. 49–52)

We in the audience share Macbeth's bitter grief because he has shared his unmitigated suffering with us. Our own judgement of

Macbeth, not just as a villain, but as a figure of supreme tragedy, is justified because of our insight into the suffering that Macbeth's implacable form of dramatic judgement carried with it from the beginning. By punishing and condemning himself Macbeth releases us from the need to do so. But none of the characters on the stage at the end shows any pity for Macbeth. They see him only as a dead butcher, as a hell-hound. And so, even in the end Macbeth remains equivocal. He is a tragic figure and a monster, fair and foul, a king and no king, still a man but less than a beast. Only after Macbeth is dead can the play's shadows of tragic equivocation be banished. 'Hail, King! for so thou art' (v. viii. 54) the victors say to Malcolm, who is King in deed as well as in name.

Apart from the psychological realities that they reflect, all the references to equivocation, to costumes, to acting, and to masks in *Macbeth* suggest to us the level of theatrical reality. In drama 'nothing is but what is not'. It is possible for a tragedy like *Macbeth* to show our eyes, and grieve our hearts. The dramatic poet himself is an equivocator, and the act of acting is itself an equivocation: the actor is and is not the character he plays. The witches who shrieked on the Elizabethan stage really were sexually ambiguous, and when Lady Macbeth asked the spirits to unsex her, the boy actor who played her part may inevitably have directed attention to the fact that on the Elizabethan stage itself Lady Macbeth always was unsexed. Similarly, Richard Burbage, playing Macbeth, was always a player-king and the 'unreal shadow' of Banquo's Ghost was embodied on the stage by an actor as corporeal as Burbage. In another illustration given for equivocation in the *Oxford English Dictionary*, Sir Thomas Browne says that 'the visible world is but a picture of the invisible, wherein as in a portrait, things are not truly, but in equivocal shapes'. Life, to Browne, is but a shadow of a higher truth. The drama itself, then, is something like a portrait, or, more accurately, something like a 'walking shadow' of the visible world, wherein, again, 'things are not truly, but in equivocal shapes'. One could argue that any time we watch a play we know that 'nothing is but what is not' and that 'things are not truly, but in equivocal shapes'. But

Macbeth is not just any play. The references and actions that stress theatrical practices are potent, and they may influence our response to the tragedy, though the precise nature of this influence seems (to me, at least) to be completely mysterious. Perhaps here, within this great tragedy of equivocation, Shakespeare simply could not resist calling attention to the equivocations inherent in his craft in order to show that if a great poet 'lies', he does indeed lie 'like truth'.

In *King Lear*, Shakespeare's great tragedy about truth and falsehood, no equivocations on the part of the characters are admitted or permitted. Like chess pieces, the characters in *King Lear* are initially divided into black ones and white ones, and they are divided according to whether they stand on the side of truth or on the side of falsehood.

> Lear. So young and so untender?
> Cordelia. So young, my lord, and true.
> (I. i. 105–6)

> Kent.   To plainness honour's bound
> When majesty falls to folly. Reserve thy state;
> And in thy best consideration check
> This hideous rashness. Answer my life my judgment:
> Thy youngest daughter does not love thee least;
> Nor are those empty-hearted whose low sounds
> Reverb no hollowness.
> (I. i. 146–52)

> Fool. They'll have me whipp'd for speaking true: thou'lt
> have me whipp'd for lying.
> (I. iv. 180–1)

The play's several spokesmen for truth are insulted, banished, stocked, tortured, and forced to go into disguise by other characters, but they nevertheless remain absolutely honest spokesmen for the truth and for the right. The liars, on the other hand, remain rich, secure, gorgeous, and powerful for a time, though the hollow falsity of all their pretensions to any form of humanity finally is dramatically exposed for ever:

> Edgar. Maugre thy strength, youth, place, and eminence,
> Despite thy victor sword and fire-new fortune,

Thy valour and thy heart—thou art a traitor;
False to thy gods, thy brother, and thy father;
Conspirant 'gainst this high illustrious prince;
And, from th'extremest upward of thy head
To the descent and dust below thy foot,
A most toad-spotted traitor.

(v. iii. 131–8)

In what is a very significant contrast to Macbeth, certain of the vicious characters in *King Lear*—Cornwall, Regan, and Goneril—suffer hardly at all before they die, and they never once condemn themselves. To the very end they remain comfortably smug in their evil. Furthermore, they experience no general recognition of the good, and they do not inevitably even face retributive justice from the good characters. Nevertheless, the vicious characters in *King Lear* are summoned to judgement, and their judgement may be the most damning of all judgements. For the deaths of Cornwall, Goneril, and Regan touch no one, on or off the stage, with any pity or awe or, indeed, with any emotion whatsoever. If Albany can dismiss the death of Edmund (who is by far the most interesting, intelligent, and sensitive villain in the play) as 'but a trifle here', the deaths of Cornwall, Goneril, and Regan are even more dismissible. So far as everybody in the theatre is concerned, their deaths are ultimately and completely insignificant. Indeed, throughout this play, Shakespeare gives these characters the emotional appeal of faceless, soulless automatons. They never come to life dramatically or emotionally. Even in their love affairs they are as malicious, cowardly, and cruel as they are when, in a group, they humiliate or torture old men:

Edmund: Yet Edmund was belov'd.
         The one the other poison'd for my sake,
         And after slew herself.
Albany.   Even so.

(v. iii. 239–41)

'Even so.' So what? There is not even any emotional interest on our parts, here, in relegating Shakespeare's goats to the eternal brimstone. They are like indistinguishable, stinging, buzzing insects (Edmund himself apparently cannot find any significant difference between Goneril and Regan), and one feels just about the same amount of emotion at their deaths as one might feel while watching the death throes of a swarm of hornets.

By contrast, the stage action '*Enter* Lear, *with* Cordelia *dead in his arms*' arouses as much human emotion as it is possible for art to elicit. However many times this play has been read, the impact of King Lear grieving over Cordelia summons forth overwhelming pity, tears, horror, the desire to help, a shriek that this cannot be, for life must not be so cruel. It arouses righteous indignation, outrage, pain, love for the old King, a complete recognition of what he must feel and a full understanding of the depth of his loss. Compared to the dramatic impact of the death of Cordelia, the deaths of a hundred Edmunds and a thousand Regans could only be considered trifles. And in spite of the fact that the death of Cordelia appears to have no significance whatsoever in terms of any gods, or any 'Absolute', the emotional responses which this death generates in the theatre and which are such completely human ones—grief, pity, love, terror—are of awesome human significance in and of themselves.

The tremendous flow of feeling which goes out to King Lear from the other characters and from the audience does not, of course, help Lear himself. Unlike Macbeth, the Lear of the last act has all that 'should accompany old age'. He has the 'honour, love, obedience, troops of friends' that Macbeth so grievously missed. But they are of no comfort to Lear bending over Cordelia. 'A plague upon you, murderers, traitors all!' he says to the characters and to the audience who have endured with him to the end. Still, the sheer humanity of Lear's fury directed against everyone who has survived his daughter only increases our pity, our understanding, our love for him. So far as we are concerned, the humane pity, the passion and the insight and the love which King Lear summons from everyone in the theatre, is *le vrai Jugement dernier*. And *King Lear* itself represents the very highest kind of art, defined by Proust as 'that which is the most real, the most austere school of life'.

Certain very austere facts of ordinary life dominate this tragedy. They are the harshest truths of human experience, and they are divorced from any of the comforts of theology or fiction. Certain good characters in the play (like Kent and Cordelia) receive no earthly reward for their loyalty, and no reward in the after-life is promised to them. If these characters are honest and true, this is because their own moral integrity requires them to be honest and to be true, and in maintaining their own moral integrity they have all the reward that they are going to get. It is also true that death is completely random, completely arbitrary. The message to the prison could have saved Cordelia. Similarly, Cornwall might have recovered from his wound. In this tragedy, we are never encouraged to consider death as a punishment for crime. Death is simply the inevitable end of life which can come, at any time, to the good and to the evil alike. Characters can therefore choose death as an escape from life whenever they wish. Gloucester constantly contemplates suicide, and Goneril commits suicide. This is one of the choices which is left to the individual characters. Another such choice is the choice of values.

On the one hand, the characters in *King Lear* may choose to adopt for themselves the values which permit human beings to live together in honour, peace, social harmony, and love:

> Good my lord,
> You have begot me, bred me, lov'd me; I
> Return those duties back as are right fit,
> Obey you, love you, and most honour you.
> Why have my sisters husbands, if they say
> They love you all? Haply, when I shall wed,
> That lord whose hand must take my plight shall carry
> Half my love with him, half my care and duty.
> Sure I shall never marry like my sisters,
> To love my father all.
>
> (I. i. 94–103)

Alternatively, the characters in this play may choose to reject all these values, and this rejection, by its very nature, clearly permits people to prey on each other like 'monsters of the deep':

> *Edmund.*   A credulous father! and a brother noble,
> Whose nature is so far from doing harms
> That he suspects none; on whose foolish honesty

> My practices ride easy! I see the business.
> Let me, if not by birth, have lands by wit:
> All with me's meet that I can fashion fit.
> (I. ii. 170-5)

> *Cornwall.*   True or false, [this letter] hath made thee Earl of Gloucester.
> (III. v. 16-17)

> *Goneril.*   . . . the laws are mine, not thine.
> Who can arraign me for't?
> (v. iii. 157-8)

Very frequently in this play the underlying motives for choosing either of these alternatives are given no dramatic importance whatsoever. It is as if Shakespeare were trying to show us that choices for right and wrong, that the deeds of good and evil based on these choices, are more important than any reasons for such choices and deeds. Remembering his experiences in German concentration camps, the psychoanalyst Bruno Bettelheim observed that 'when the chips were down it was utterly unimportant why a person acted the way he did; the only thing that counted was how he acted'.[15] Similarly, in the crisis situations of *King Lear*, we judge the characters completely on the basis of the decisions that they make and act upon, and the reasons for their decisions or actions are of no great concern to us.

Certainly no gods in this tragedy will intervene to prevent the rejection of all humane[16] values, nor will they intervene to punish those who reject these values. The only evil, the only justice, the only mercy, and the only miracles that occur in this play result from the actions of men. We see that the monsters who prey on others may finally turn on each other and kill each other off, just as Goneril kills Regan. We see that honourable men like Edgar may finally rise to fight against evil. But these fates, these facts, obviously reflect the very common human consequences of very common human evil. They do not (necessarily) reflect some

---

[15] Bruno Bettelheim, *The Informed Heart* (London, 1970), p. 25.

[16] Sir Peter Medawar's dictionary definition of 'humane' seems as good a definition as any: '"humaneness", according to the dictionary, means "characterized by such behaviour or disposition towards others as befits a man"' (*The Future of Man* (London, 1960), p. 56).

Divine Judgement in favour of the good. Similarly, the bonds which hold society together—the values of kinship, honesty, friendship, loyalty, kindness, and love—are very basic social values. No supernatural sanction is given to them. To choose to abide by them is, in *King Lear*, to choose full humanity, but this choice (given the fact that other human beings are perfectly free to behave in monstrous ways) will not preclude cruel suffering. It may in fact increase it. Certainly, within their dramatic life-times the good characters in *King Lear* suffer more, not less, than the evil ones. Indeed, taking a stand for moral and social order, in this play, is consistently shown to be harder and more dangerous than deliberately rejecting any social or moral obligations that might interfere with self-interest. To tell the truth, to do one's moral or social duty to others, is to face banishment, torture, or death:

> *Lear.*   Kent, on thy life, no more!
> *Kent.*   My life I never held but as a pawn
>   To wage against thine enemies; nor fear to lose it,
>   Thy safety being motive.
>
> (I. i. 153–6)

> *Gloucester.* If I die for it, as no less is threatened me, the King my old master must be relieved.
>
> (III. iii. 17–19)

> *Cordelia.*   No blown ambition doth our arms incite,
>   But love, dear love, and our ag'd father's right.
>
> (IV. iv. 27–8)

Kent, Gloucester, Cordelia, the Fool, and others decide to take their stands at great cost to their personal safety and comfort. And if, as this play suggests that it may be, death is the death-obliterate and not necessarily the entrance to another form of life, then the characters who choose the good are treated far more cruelly by Shakespeare himself than the characters who choose evil, since they suffer so much before they die. On the other hand, the good characters do all come to life before they die. They help each other, they can trust each other, they all finally give or finally receive unconditional love, and they go down as human beings who have taken a stand on the side of humane values. In a moving account of the prisoners whose integrity triumphed over all the horrors of Dachau and Buchenwald, Bruno Bettelheim gives us a keen insight into the brave stands taken by the good characters in *King Lear*:

. . . to survive as a man not a walking corpse, as a debased and degraded but still human being, one had first and foremost to remain informed and aware of what made up one's personal point of no return, the point beyond which one would never, under any circumstances, give in to the oppressor, even if it meant risking and losing one's life. It meant being aware that if one survived at the price of overreaching this point one would be holding on to a life that had lost all its meaning. It would mean surviving—not with a lowered self-respect, but without any.[17]

By taking their stands on the side of moral and social order, Kent, Cordelia, Gloucester, Edgar, and the Fool claim for themselves and (so far as the audience is concerned) they ultimately inherit the kingdom of humanity which the banally portrayed villains, the play's 'walking corpses', never even enter. At their most debased and degraded, the good characters remain human beings, not beasts, while their rich, secure persecutors are metaphorically identified with the lowest forms of life on the play's evolutionary scale.

Interestingly, if obviously, in the beginning of the play, Edmund seems far more interesting than Edgar. Thereafter, however, while Edmund never (until his one attempt at a good deed in the end) deviates from his originally defined bastardy, Edgar goes (and grows) through a series of drastic mutations. He goes all the way down to Poor Turlygood, poor Tom ('Edgar I nothing am') and then—always serving his father—he moves up to his triumphant victory as the (literally and figuratively) 'true' son and heir of the Earl of Gloucester who is able to recognize evil and overcome it. Gloucester himself, in the beginning, is callow and crass. His first real moral commitment costs him his eyes. But Gloucester does learn to 'see', because he learns to 'feel' (IV. i.

---

[17] *The Informed Heart*, pp. 145–6.

69–70), while he was able to do neither in the opening scenes of the play. Gloucester finally dies a death which combines the two ultimate human passions, the extremes of joy and sorrow. When he experienced them, his heart 'burst smilingly'. And that is not the worst way for a man to die.

Lear, of course, goes through the greatest mutation of all. He begins as a petty old tyrant who flings away love and integrity and truth as if he were unloading counterfeit money. But Lear ends his life as 'the King himself'. Precisely how Lear feels when he dies will always remain a great dramatic mystery, but there is never any question where he dies. To that question, everybody in the theatre can only answer in the words of Kent, 'In your own kingdom, Sir'. By the end of the play Lear deserves all the love and the respect he wanted so much at the beginning. He has learned to know himself utterly ('Forget and forgive, I am old and foolish'), and where he once insisted upon being protected and pitied, Lear learns to pity and to protect others at some of the very darkest moments in his life. He pities his Fool in the storm (III. ii. 66–73) and he comforts Cordelia on their way to prison. There is no doubt that this mighty old man 'might have saved' his daughter if only Shakespeare had let him get there in time. Shakespeare himself sends King Lear out into the tempest and then forces Lear to experience all the worst things that a man can experience, and King Lear endures to the end. For this reason, Lear is the greatest of Shakespeare's dramatic affirmations of the human capacity to grow, to learn, to feel, and to remain an unconditionally royal lord of earth in spite of all the physical suffering human beings may share with the humblest animals, and in spite of experiencing a degree of emotional suffering which no animal can know.

And this is why, despite all the justifiable intellectual arguments that *King Lear* makes a grotesque mockery of human aspirations set against an indifferent and absurd Absolute, the play still, to the common reader, represents an affirmation of the human capacity to surmount all inhuman indifference, all absurdity. We ourselves, as human beings watching Shakespeare's great tragedy, cannot be indifferent to the King Lear of the final acts, nor does

Lear ever seem to us (even in his most grotesque moments) merely an illustration of life's absurdity. We cannot even remain indifferent to his followers. Shakespeare will not permit us to do so. Certainly he makes everyone in the audience feel the highest admiration for Kent, who never once requests any admiration from anyone, but who categorically, by word and by deed, defines himself as a man:

> *Lear.* What art thou?
> *Kent.* A man, sir.
> *Lear.* What dost thou profess? What wouldst thou with us?
> *Kent.* I do profess to be no less than I seem, to serve him truly that will put me in trust, to love him that is honest, to converse with him that is wise and says little, to fear judgment, to fight when I cannot choose . . .
>
> (I. iv. 9–17)

Kent never expects any reward for being 'a man'. His unselfishly loyal service to the King is never fully recognized by Lear. But it is recognized by the audience. From their point of view, Kent dares do 'all that doth become a man'. He never compromises with his integrity—with his truth to himself or his truth to others. He takes a firm stand against evil. He loves, he serves. He is one of the characters who literally and figuratively inherits the kingdom in the end, and 'Who will inherit the kingdom?' is perhaps the most crucial question raised, and answered, throughout this play.

Obviously, by any standards of calculated self-interest, Kent is a complete fool. The Fool himself makes this clear. But the Fool also makes it clear that those who subordinate everything to self-interest are knaves who, in the long run, will prove to be even greater fools:

> That sir which serves and seeks for gain,
>   And follows but for form,
> Will pack when it begins to rain,
>   And leave thee in the storm.
> But I will tarry; the fool will stay
>   And let the wise man fly.
> The knave turns fool that runs away;
>   The fool no knave, perdy.
>
> (II. iv. 76–83)

In the last analysis, by his treatment and judgement of the characters in *King Lear*, Shakespeare makes the conventional worldly wisdom of the vicious characters appear ultimately foolish. And their selfishness appears supremely foolish in terms of the most basic standards by which common humanity evaluates the quality of human life. Kent's life has human value and significance. The life of Regan does not.

For if men like Lear, Kent, Edgar, and the Fool are faced not only by human evil, but by an indifferent universe as well, then they can, they must, help each other to surmount this indifference. Indeed, in this play, they are obliged to do so in order to give meaning to their own lives and to the lives of others. Clearly the only meaning they can give to life is a human meaning. The storm does not care whether or not it is afflicting King Lear. Kent does care. Because the characters cannot expect intervention from any Absolute, it is up to them to create their own heavens or hells, their own kingdoms, on earth. The universe, the world, the stage of all human actions, permits all forms of life to occupy it. It impartially allows the existence of the highest and the lowest forms of life—toads, monsters of the deep, and men. The sun, the storms, the universe which these forms of life inhabit, appear to be completely neutral towards them all. So there is no point in either blaming the universe for not abiding by specifically human values, or blaming it for human failures to abide by them:

> This is the excellent foppery of the world, that, when we are sick in fortune, often the surfeits of our own behaviour, we make guilty of our disasters the sun, the moon, and stars; as if we were villains on necessity; fools by heavenly compulsion; knaves, thieves, and treachers, by spherical predominance; drunkards, liars, and adulterers, by an enforc'd obedience of planetary influence; and all that we are evil in, by a divine thrusting on . . .
>
> (I. ii. 110–20)

Writing about the future of man, Sir Peter Medawar concludes that men have been passing responsibility for their own actions to some metaphysical force or other for too long:

> Think only of what we have suffered from a belief in the existence and overriding authority of a fighting instinct; from the doctrines of

racial superiority and the metaphysics of blood and soil; from the belief that warfare between men or classes of men or nations represents a fulfilment of historical laws. These are all excuses of one kind or another, and pretty thin excuses. The inference we can draw from an analytical study of the differences between ourselves and other animals is surely this: that the bells which toll for mankind are—most of them, anyway—like the bells on Alpine cattle; they are attached to our own necks, and it must be *our* fault if they do not make a cheerful and harmonious sound.[18]

We can draw precisely the same inference from Shakespeare's analytical study of the differences between men (who can choose to be good or evil) and animals (to whom the human definitions of good and evil do not apply) throughout *King Lear*. In no other play by Shakespeare is the 'scene' of so little influence on the characters. The great stage of the world, in this play, is only a stage, a setting for human actions. A court can be the scene where deeds of great virtue or great viciousness are acted out by men. So can a heath. A castle can be a refuge or a torture chamber, entirely depending on how people behave within it. So can a hovel. How people act, how they treat each other, is all that matters.

How people act, how they treat each other, is all that matters, also, in the last judgement issued in the New Testament: 'I was hungry and you fed me.' Time after time, in so many great works of the human intellect, traditionally 'divine' truths and judgements turn out to be the basic human truths and judgements. These works, these truths, do have a kind of divinity, because they have a universality (so far as human experience is concerned) that transcends time, space, and all the convulsive changes in theological dogma and intellectual fashion. For instance, whoever speaks the epilogue to *King Lear* appears to use the universally inclusive 'we' (as well as the royal 'we') when he says it is imperative that, at whatever cost, people speak the truth:

> The weight of this sad time we must obey;
> Speak what we feel, not what we ought to say.

And certainly the very greatest artists, philosophers, and scientists have always told the truth as they felt and saw it, no matter what

[18] *The Future of Man*, p. 103.

their historical situations may have told them that they 'ought to say'. And with astonishing frequency they independently arrive at exactly the same conclusions. Over and over again they give us the same truths. Maybe this is another reason why certain truths have taken on a numen—they frequently come from the most intelligent and the most sensitive human beings that have spoken to other human beings over the centuries. But the main reason they survive so triumphantly is surely because they *are* truths. Many of the inferences arrived at in *King Lear*, for instance, are arrived at by quite a different route in the following quotation from Proust's *The Captive*:

> All that we can say is that everything is arranged in this life as though we entered it carrying the burden of obligations contracted in a former life; there is no reason inherent in the conditions of life on this earth that can make us consider ourselves obliged to do good, to be fastidious, to be polite even, nor make the talented artist consider himself obliged to begin over again a score of times a piece of work the admiration aroused by which will matter little to his body devoured by worms, like the patch of yellow wall painted with so much knowledge and skill by an artist who must for ever remain unknown and is barely identified under the name Vermeer. All these obligations which have not their sanction in our present life seem to belong to a different world, founded upon kindness, scrupulosity, self-sacrifice, a world entirely different from this, which we leave in order to be born into this world, before perhaps returning to the other to live once again beneath the sway of those unknown laws which we have obeyed because we bore their precepts in our hearts, knowing not whose hand had traced them there—those laws to which every profound work of the intellect brings us nearer and which are invisible only—and still!—to fools.[19]

The fact that Shakespeare dramatically exhibits his truths about human values by showing human beings in a world without any divine order, while Proust feels that the identical human values may ultimately reflect some divine order, does not matter. The truths hurled out at us by both artists are the same. And if Shakespeare and Proust permit us, in very differing ways, to know, to

[19] Marcel Proust, *The Captive*, trans. C. K. Scott Moncrieff (New York, 1932), pp. 509–10.

see, to feel, their truths, then their works have done all that human art—the living likeness of truth that transcends the artist's time and space—ever can do for us. Whether or not we consider ourselves obliged to act upon these truths remains our own affair.

Index